VITAMIN
G
GRATITUDE

The Daily Supplement to
create a magical Life
of Fulfilment you deserve

**42 Grateful Living Practices for Joy, Abundance,
and Resilience in less than 5-minutes a day.**

BY

PRASHANT JAIN

DEDICATION

Dedicated to my daughter Anamika Jain
My biggest challenge and my greatest blessing

VITAMIN G: GRATITUDE

*The daily supplement to create
the magical life you deserve*

Prashant Jain

*42 Grateful Living Practices for Joy, Abundance,
and Resilience in less than 5-minutes a day.*

First print edition in India published by :
BSC Publishers & Distributors
Digital version by : The Seed of Gratitude

the seed of
GRATITUDE

Cover design by the Author

Available at all leading Book Stores
E-Book at http://www.vitamingratitude.com
Kindle from Amazon.com

ACKNOWLEDGEMENTS

To my parents Vastimal Jain and Ratan Devi My family in Guntur and Rajasthan

To my Editors Mona Ramavat, Manjiri Ganu, Narayanan Ganeshan.

To Suresh VMRG for the amazing layout design of this book.

To Ananth Vardhan, The Typewriter Effect, for the design of the characters and resources in this book.

To Poosapati Parameshwar Raju for the logo of Gratitude Flower.

To Megha Dinesh for the enhancements and constant feedback.

To my teachers Nithya Shanti, Sujith Ravindran, Sadguru Jaggi Vasudev, Sat and Siri Puran Singh Khalsa for inspiring me and putting me on to the path of gratitude.

To the pioneers and ambassadors who have contributed to the field of gratitude: Robert Emmons, Dalai Lama, Oprah Winfrey, Anthony Robbins and Brother David Steindl-Rast among many others, whose ground-breaking work and trust in the practice of gratitude have inspired me and opened the doors to my own self-exploration.

To my teams at CtrlS Datacenters Ltd, Gifting Happiness Pvt Ltd, Meghavi Wellness, India Domain, The Seed of Gratitude foundation

To the many people from my life and work who have been a part of the Circle of Gratitude - the Facebook group I started in 2016, in which thousands of people have tried these gratitude practices and shared their experiences of real life transformation resulting from the 365-day gratitude and daily challenges. They have been the focus group for testing each gratitude practice and have contributed through their stories inputs, feedback.

PRAISE FOR VITAMIN G GRATITUDE

Beyond the usual gratitude journal, lists, stone and jar, Vitamin G shifts the bar towards quick, easy and workable idea for new age and millennial generation.

A heart touching book on living a grateful life.

I always used to crib about the entitlement that people have and how they take everything for granted, this book gave me an insight that was life changing.

A book for my bedside that I can refer again and again whenever I'm feeling negative, complaining or dissatisfied to shift myself towards gratitude.

Prashant's journey and transformation through gratitude is amazing.

Easy and ready reckoner of gratitude practices.

Loved the interactive nature of the book and all the 5-minute exercises.

Learning the fine art of praising and appreciating others.

Was a eye opener and shifted my understanding of gratitude as a transaction.

Cleared the myth in my mind that I was also thankful.

It taught why the secret had not worked for and what to do to truly manifest abundance.

My relationship is more connected and I sleep better.

I was able to help my kids understand the value of gratitude better with vitamin G.

The only page I read was the reverse bucket list and my mindset of only looking at dream and plans was a revelation.

On a spiritual path for over a decade I thought I was very grateful person till I read this book and the multiple ways in which gratitude could be practiced till it becomes our very being.

The no complaint gratitude band revealed to me how much complaining I was.

In a world of life coaches, PJ is the gratitude guru for sure.

It's the best gift book I got which helped me understand how gratitude can help me be happier and joyful.

Very easy to read and apply to relationships.

Applied some of the idea to my office and definitely there was a feel good factor.

Gratitude did cure my insomnia, now I count my blessing.

Gratitude is now really my attitude. Thank you, Prashant.

Deepened my understanding of how to handle ingratitude.

Gratitude is the best thing that happened to me, Thank you for bringing it my life.

"Vitamin G has the power to Transform life" - The Times of India.

With deft visuals the book is an easy read - but use it like a manual to work through it. At Rs 295, it won't pinch. Who knows, you may be grateful for the opportunity to spend the money to buy it! And then reap the bounty of gratitude! – Deccan Chronicle

Through stories, humour, exercises, reflections and 42 simple, easy to integrate gratitude practices, it covers all aspects of our life like relationships, health, happiness, work, prosperity and abundance, – Indian Express

The book 'Vitamin G — Gratitude' by Prashant Jain speaks about the vitamin that helps us in creating a magical life – The Hindu.

MISSION BILLION THANKS
Foreword by Prashant Jain

In the year 1999, when I was 24, I sold my first company, IndiaDomain.com to Asia Online, funded by Softbank and JP Morgan, for a Million USD. Between 2005 and 2008, I was diagnosed with depression and survived two suicide attempts. I had almost no money left and hardly any friends. Totally down in the dumps and unable to pull myself up, I turned to self-help books and became a new age workshop junkie, exploring every psychometric assessment and went on to explore a path of seeking and spirituality.

In 2009, the idea of practicing gratitude in everyday life found me and had stayed with me ever since. Cut to 2015 and I am running four companies with a turnover in millions and have several friends, a healthy mind and body with joy being the undercurrent of my life. Through all of this abundance, the true realization of success came to me by just being in the gratitude vibration and living gratefully.

In 2016, I met Dalai Lama and took on the Mission Billion Thanks - A mission for dedicating my life to amplify the vibration of gratitude on the planet.

Over the last seven years, I have been working on myself by practicing gratitude in my personal life, with other people on social media and at work. I have been holding workshops and corporate seminars, and work with various groups and communities with the endeavor to plant the seed of gratitude.

From journaling to carrying a gratitude stone (I have had one in my wallet since 2009), experimenting with various campaigns on social media, it has been a remarkable journey of transformation for me and for people around me. In one of my experiments of appreciating anyone who tagged himself on my Facebook wall, authentically, genuinely and specifically, had me online on a 48 hour marathon. Birthday celebrations at my workplace turned into a Public Display of Appreciation practice for the colleague whose birthday it was. For years, I have worked on the gratitude week in multiple organizations - some as large as having 5000 employees - to help incorporate the culture of gratitude within the organization. Every conversation with different teachers and leaders I met eventually steered towards gratitude and its true nature.

For months now, in the Circle of Gratitude, many people have practiced the grateful living practices in this book and offered their transformative experiences to help fine tune them.

This book is a part of these experiences and hundreds of personal and community initiatives that have blossomed as a part of Mission Billion Thanks.

This is the seed of gratitude I offer to you. May it become a forest of thankfulness in our world through you.

My wish for you from this book

By making the choice to read this book, you have chosen to magnify gratitude in your world. Thank you for that. Here is my wish and prayer:

May this book help you in:

- Using as many or all of the of 42 practices
- Reflecting upon and using the interactive pages
- Expanding your ideas about gratitude after reading about how it has transformed my life, which I hope will trigger your own thoughts and emotions.

I ardently wish that you bring the transformative magical power of gratitude to your life through at least one quality, practice or idea from this book to apply to your life.

As you begin to read this book, I am tempted to quote Joseph Brodsky, one of the most profound writers that I have come across who very brilliantly describes how books and their insights affect us:

And at the moment of reading, you become what you read
You become the state of the language, which is a poem
And it's epiphany, or its revelation is yours
They are still yours once you shut the book
Since you can't revert to not having had them
That's what evolution is all about

It is my sincere hope and blessing that may you evolve into deep gratitude, May you be grateful. For gratitude, in my humble opinion, is the offering of our purest self-expression that radiates from our core and propels us towards self-actualization.

THE LEGION OF GRATEFULNESS

The 6A Framework Of Connecting To Gratitude©

ATTENTION	AWARENESS	ACTION	APPRECIATION	ACCEPTANCE	ACTUALIZATION
Master Phontastic	Dr. Big Head	Major Strong	Mr. Expressive	Ms. Wonder	Brother Monk

Knowing	Thinking	Doing	Expressing	Feeling	Being

© 2017 Prashant Jain & The Seed of Gratitude

TABLE OF CONTENTS

PART 1 : **A**TTENTION
KNOWING

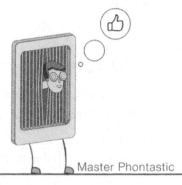

Master Phontastic

THE LIFE TRANSFORMING
MAGIC OF GRATITUDE

Chapters

Connecting to Gratitude

Beyond Indebtedness and Transaction

Reciprocation, Obligation and Mirroring

Multivitamin of Benefits

Gratosphere of 360 Gratitude

Gratitude Sans Expectations

The Forest of Gratefulness

THE LIFE TRANSFORMING MAGIC OF GRATITUDE

Practices

Wheel of Life Gratefulness

Gratitude Journal

Four Portals of Gratitude

Morning Rituals

Gratitude Zones

Gratitude Inventory

Life as a Gratitude Festival

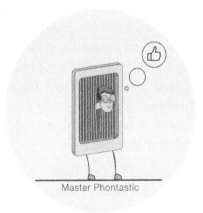

Master Phontastic

1

CONNECTING TO GRATITUDE

A book for the millennial times that makes you interact by knowing, thinking, reflecting, feeling, saying, doing, practicing in a focused, quick and easy way such that it changes your being.

By the age of 24, I sold my first web services company for a million US Dollars. Over the next few years, three events changed my life and the world around me forever. The first was the dot-com bust in 2000, second was the stock market crash, and third the 9/11 attacks. In a few years, I went from being the poster boy of ecommerce and celebrated everywhere for my success to being bankrupt, clinically depressed and suicidal in 2005. These years of adversity and major life challenges till 2009 put me on a path of gratitude and grateful living. Today, I run multiple companies in technology, gifting, training and wellness, living a joyful life of abundance, contentment and fulfillment in my being, my health, relationships and work.

This book is my loving gift to share insights, practices and moments from my life on how gratitude has transformed me from a depressive pessimist to the joy-filled person that I am today. I have come across several unconditionally grateful people who I draw inspiration from. I have made it the purpose of my life to magnify joy by raising my gratitude consciousness. Deepening the practice of gratitude can rewire the brain towards positivity and optimism, the heart towards kindness and acceptance, and expression towards appreciation. Gratitude gives us the resilience to face life's major challenges and obstacles that come in our path.

As a child, I learnt moral gratitude and good behavior as taught by my parents, of saying thank you for the toys and chocolates I received and being a 'good boy' by sharing till it became an automatic unconscious habit, at times not even heartfelt. As a teenager I learnt to negotiate with God, masquerading my needs, wants, requisitions as prayers, giving offerings and trading in gratitude. As an adult in an office environment, I learnt the transactional gratitude; scared of receiving, fearing that I would have to return those favors out of obligation, feeling the need to mirror and reciprocate. I struggled for almost a decade, confusing indebtedness for gratitude unaware of non-transactional gratitude or gratitude that is simply felt, without expectations. I am still not there yet, but strive every day to get to that place of higher gratitude vibration than I was, the previous day.

The 42 gratitude practices come out of my own experiments, experiences, observations, deepening my practices, learning, and teaching over a decade. Most of them require less than five minutes of investment per day with the potential to becoming life-long habits and a way of being and living gratefully.

The book is divided into 6 parts with 7 chapters in each: Based on 6A framework that I have devised and used as gratitude coach in my retreats, grateful workplaces and business transformation exercises, Knowing (Attention), Thinking (Awareness), Feeling (Acceptance), Expressing (Appreciation), Doing (Action) and Being (Actualization).

The number 42 here is a sly reference to Douglas Adams' book, The Hitchhikers Guide to the Galaxy. Type "what's the answer to the universe and everything" on Google and you'll get 42 as the answer. Google too seems to love Douglas Adams' sense of humor, just like I do. I wish to contribute to the world by bringing awareness to practicing gratitude so much that it echoes within humanity and creates ripples that touch as many lives as possible.

Pick any of these 42 seeds of gratitude, sow them in your heart, and nurture them to create your own magnificent forest of thankfulness. Begin with taking a view of your life Gratefulness.

Practice: Wheel of Life Gratefulness

Take an inventory of your life by using the Wheel of Life Gratefulness practice. This is your symbolic step towards creating a happy and grateful life. This 5-minute task is a great tool to balance your life every week/month/ quarterly.

List what you are grateful for in all six areas. Describe how you feel about the things you've listed. How much do they mean to you? What impact do they have on your life?

Some areas might be difficult to list blessings for. Focus on that area of your life where you are currently facing challenges in, to find at least a few blessings. As you move into the gratitude mode, you will find more blessings in those areas through the practices and insights from this book, and the wheel of life gratefulness will expand.

WHEEL
OF
LIFE GRATEFULNESS

Write in each quadrant of the circle things that you are thankful for. For more than four items in a particular segment of your life, use additional sheet.

21

2

BEYOND INDEBTEDNESS
AND TRANSACTION

Gratitude cannot be a transaction or a bribery born out of expectations; it is the expression of our true thankful nature.

Growing up in a rather typical upper middle class Indian family, I, like most children, knew that saying, 'thank you' could earn me the approval of my parents and elders, make me come across as a 'good' boy and generally be considered as well-mannered. At the work place across my various jobs in US and India, thanking people around me soon turned into a subconscious habit of ego-boosting with no real feelings associated with it, as was the case with most of my colleagues. This 'scratch-my-back-and-I'll-scratch-yours' mindset and doing things based on obligations and expectations was what I had learnt and experienced as gratitude, all through my life.

It is easy to mistake gratitude for a social idea of indebtedness or a means to get something. How many times have we struck a deal with god himself, offering gratitude in exchange for our desires to be fulfilled?

Gratitude is not an investment that you offer to God and the universe, or merely a tool for wish manifestation, as prescribed in several popular books like The Secret by Rhonda Byrne. Instead, it is something you offer without expectations, with the awareness that your true nature is abundance.

The essence of gratitude is captured by the very elements that it is not. Let's not confuse indebtedness with gratitude. The rhythm of silence is in the absence of sound. You can experience its overflowing presence only when noise is unable to manifest its toehold on our senses. Only when we move beyond the ideas of transactional and conditioned responses, from obligation or reciprocation, can we get to the true meaning of gratitude.

Gratitude is essentially the recognition of the unearned increments of value in one's experience - the positive things that come our way that we did not actively work towards or seek. The word 'gratitude' comes from its Latin root, grata or gratia - a given gift - and from the same root comes the word, grace, which refers to a gift freely given. Far from being a passive temporary emotion, gratitude is an active, energizing force with the power to change life from lack to abundance, complaining to appreciating, and emptiness to fulfillment.

Interestingly, along with pleasant and positive feelings that come up as you go about practicing gratitude, you may also experience some unpleasant feelings. I have - like many others that I've worked with - experienced feelings of discomfort, awkwardness and even guilt in the beginning. This is perfectly natural. Many of us start to feel pressurised to repay in equal measure or more of what we have received, or feel uncomfortable about asking for something in the first place. We tend to feel guilty about not thanking 'soon enough' or 'well enough'. I have found that a good way to deal with such feelings when they surface is to stay with them rather than resist them, and gently remind yourself that gratitude is not indebtedness. They will eventually ebb away, giving way to a more uplifting experience of appreciation and joy.

Gratitude is in knowing peace of mind and contentment against the greed of hoarding and over-indulgence.

Gratitude is in feeling the abundance within so that the ephemeral nature of our existence and our dependence on things beyond our control stop mattering so much.

Gratitude is in finding true self-expression of our gifts, blessings, talents and skills so that our giving can amplify happiness and joy.

Practice: Gratitude Journal

Gratitude journaling helps us improve the overall quality of life. Write about things that are going right in your life. Maintain a daily, weekly or biweekly routine of writing for about 5 minutes.

To begin with, write down 3, 5, or 10 things that you are grateful for in a day or week. Savor the writing rather than rushing through. You could use a diary, logbook, notepad, an app, or even pieces of loose paper.

Note the things you are grateful for and visualize your thankfulness. Include even the smallest of things you feel good and grateful about; from the mundane or every day to something inspiring and big and things you take for granted. Use the template provided which is designed based on proven scientific research.

Date: ....

I am Thankful/Grateful /Happy for

- ....
- ....
- ....

How can I make this day great?

- ....
- ....
- ....

Affirmations of Thankfulness - I am

- I am ....
- I am ....
- I am ....

What can be joyfully improved today?

- ....
- ....
- ....

Use a notebook, buy a special diary, use any journaling app, or photocopy the above and write either before you go to sleep, or just after you get up. Handwritten journals improve the quality of life in areas of health, relationships, abundance.

3

RECIPROCATION, OBLIGATION AND MIRRORING

Reciprocity and obligations come from a pro-social construct and are characteristics of indebtedness.

From being steeped in depression and on the brink of suicide several years ago, to today, when I am grateful for every moment of my life, the journey has been deeply transformative. After ravenously reading up many books on positive thinking and attending a flurry of workshops, I was still quite stuck where I was with not much difference in my life. I hardly had any money, friends and had several health issues. It was easy to simply give up on life.

And then one day, I decided that I was grateful simply for being alive. Gradually, that feeling of thankfulness extended to my parents and family, and eventually to everyone and everything. Today, I live a more joyful and fulfilled life. The decision to choose grateful living was the critical internal shift that has changed my life completely.

Gratitude is not just a happy feeling, but also gives a wholesome sense of peace and contentment with everything around you.

When you start nurturing gratitude within you, it will attract immense positive energy into all areas of your life.

The pro-social behavior of animals and humans comes from our heritage of finding strength in numbers, groups, tribes and societies for survival, depending on mirroring and reciprocating to survive and thrive.

Sometimes we do things from the perspective of right and wrong, duty, morality, obligation, reciprocation and fear instead of love. Even receiving favors can make us feel obligated and guilty, considering it as a burden of debt to be returned as soon as possible. Gratitude isn't born of guilt, it is born of overwhelming joy of having received something unexpected over and above our expectation and it is given without any expectation of returning favors.

When was the last time you felt an unconditional overwhelming feeling of gratitude at something that you received for free, when you least expected it and was definitely unearned?

When did a child or a pet evoke in you a deep nurturing spirit and the urge to give unconditional love to someone, anyone?

When did an act of compassion and kindness by another human being bring to you the truth, awareness and understanding of your own ability to contribute?

We have all experienced these feelings and situations at some point. These are expressions of the gratitude vibration. If practiced long enough, gratitude can turn into a way of life, wherein you are grateful for everything - your achievements and your gifts, life's blessings and every relationship. Yes, it is totally possible and doable; the transformation comes about bit by bit, day by day, if you consistently practice. We have inherited the idea of gratitude as a way of life from our ancestors over countless generations, going beyond cultures and eras. Embedded in our collective consciousness and wisdom, gratitude as a value already exists within us. It is only a matter of realizing it ourselves to get back in touch with this wonderful vibration.

The shift from a mindset locked in complaining, cribbing, negativity and victimhood to that of appreciation, contentment and joy can be brought about gradually and in small but meaningful ways. It takes a small first step to begin, regardless of where you are currently in your personal journey. What helped me in recognizing the four portals of gratitude - blessings, learning, mercies, and protection - was a monthly exercise of focusing on the areas of health, finances, relationships and work as mentioned in the award-winning author, educator, and corporate consultant - Angeles Arrien's highly recommended book "Living in Gratitude".

Practice: Four Portals of Gratitude by Angeles Arrien

This practice is a reflection and can be done on paper or in your mind every week/month/quarter.

1) Gifts and Blessings: What major blessings have you received and given? Who or what has inspired you?

2) Learnings: What major learnings have you received and given? Who/what is challenging you?

3) Mercies: What were the mercies you have received today? What major mercies have you received and given? Who or what is surprising you?

4) Protections: The instinct to protect our self is inherent to all humans. What were the protections you have received and given?

These reflections should give you an idea of what is strengthening, opening and deepening within your being.

GRATITUDE ISN'T A BOOMERANG

Indebtedness demands an echo   *Gratitude is a ripple*

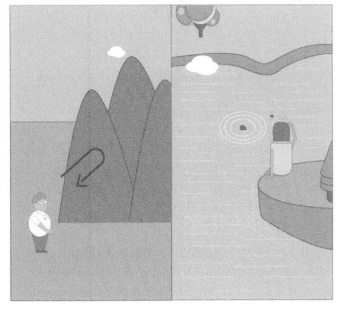

Expecting others to respond sooner or later is assuming indebtedness on the part of others. Gratitude is a ripple that traverses the Universe and touches many lives.

4

MULTIVITAMIN OF BENEFITS

Gratitude is the teflon to face life's challenges and strengthens our immunity against hardships.

When I was clinically diagnosed with depression, I was put on heavy anti-depressants, steroids and sleep medication, which was altering the neurochemistry of my body but wasn't doing much to my mindset. I discovered the idea of gratitude as being more than a mere feeling; it influenced me at different levels - body, mind, heart and soul. It changed my beliefs, opening my heart to life.

I have been nurturing myself every day ever since with gratitude which is an amalgamation of various positive feelings, choices, attitudes and qualities. And therefore, I would like to call it a multivitamin. It is made up of compassion, appreciation, thankfulness, generosity and many other such positive emotions. Which positive feelings would you like to add to your own personal composition of gratitude?

I ultimately made a choice to start living a life that involved more thankfulness and less complaining. It started to reflect in almost everything that I was doing, every task of the day, regardless of how seemingly small or big it was. You can choose to be grateful or ungrateful. Every moment of every day of your life offers that choice.

The morning ritual exercise presented with this chapter is something that immensely helped me make that choice. There was a time when I was addicted to my phone, the number of likes on my Facebook status would determine my mood. Over time, I turned my morning ritual to not check my phone, instead check with myself on what my blessings were. It turned out to be a truly liberating exercise for me.

Rather than jumping straight into your to-do-lists, and starting your day on a note of anxiety, why not wake up to a ritual of counting what you are genuinely thankful for. It can be a motivating and inspiring start to the day to launch into joyful improvement and action from a place of love and abundance rather than fear and inadequacy. Think of gratitude as Vitamin G and ask, 'Have you had your daily dose?' A life of gratitude is about finding opportunities to thank people, situations and circumstances.

Kabir, one of the greatest poets of Indian sufi and bhakti tradition says:

'In anguish everyone prays to Him, in joy does none
To One who prays in happiness, How can sorrow come'

Gratitude is similar. We should exercise it as an emotional muscle during our good times so that we can develop the resilience to face any bad times. Vitamin G improves our immunity to face life's challenges and the stress in everyday life. We develop resilience to handle adversities, be it financial issues, health problems or relationship troubles. Besides these, immediate benefits like better sleep and a higher pain threshold are guaranteed as it increases our satisfaction levels and feeling of contentment with where we are.

Grateful living gets us into an appreciation mode with everyone around us as we recognize our interdependence with people. This expression of thankfulness for our inter-connectedness, bonds us better, strengthens our relationships and helps nurture them in an appreciative and joyful manner.

Just like the body needs exercise to be healthy, our muscle of gratitude too needs to be flexed regularly. The more you mindfully practice gratitude by taking every opportunity to thank someone or something that has added value to your life, the more you are strengthening the gratitude muscle. It can maximize our life satisfaction and the quality of our life by making us optimistic, less consumerist, peaceful and joyful.

Practice: Morning Rituals

I use the moments before fully waking up to focus on and think of things that I am grateful for from yesterday and for the coming day. From all areas of my life, I count at least three specific or generic blessings and visualize them by expressing silent gratitude before I get up.

This conscious shifting of my mind towards positivity and grateful optimism is a gratitude morning ritual I have followed for years.

This gives a super charged positive head start to the day and rewires our brain to gratitude in under a minute.

You could also put your ten fingertips together in a lotus position. Visualize and count ten things you are grateful for by parting each finger in tandem. These may be situations, qualities, people or things.

GRATITUDE
DAILY
DOSE

DID YOU TAKE YOUR
VITAMIN GRATITUDE TODAY?

RELIEVES SYMPTOMS OF

Complaining
Cribbing
Cursing
Entitlement
Taking for Granted
Scarcity

DETOX FROM

Negativity
Excessive needs and Desires
Gossip
Envy and Pride
Me me
Fear

SOUL SUPPLEMENTS FOR

Mental balance
Physical well being
Emotional vibrance
Enhanced quality of life

A morning dose of gratitude will give the strength and power required to face life with kindness, compassion, grace, generosity, positivity and optimism.

33

5

GRATOSPHERE 360 GRATITUDE

*As you expand your sphere of gratefulness,
the universe embraces you more.*

A few years back before Uber started operations in our city, some of the taxi drivers would not keep their cars or themselves clean, would be rude, insensitive to passenger needs and impolite. After the rating system was introduced and reviews started coming in, I would often be asked for a rating; in fact in a year, the cars were cleaner, the behavior became polite and professional with an improved sensitivity towards passenger needs. It was a rating system of thankfulness so that people could share word of mouth references for great service. With the advent of social media, apps and forced ratings and reviews, the enforced gratitude had changed behavior just like it did for us in our childhood.

Ratings, reviews of thankfulness - like with taxi or food delivery apps - and words of appreciation are a way of steering yourself towards practicing gratitude. Applied previously in several areas, including the hospitality industry, these rating systems are proven to have brought about tremendous improvements in the quality of service.

Gratosphere refers to the extent to which our gratitude spreads. It is made of seven circles - the self, immediate family, close friends, extended family, workplace, community, nation and the world. Today, with boundaries blurring between nations and cultures, personal and workspaces, family and friends, we live in a world of interdependence. Our gratosphere extends from us, eventually encompassing the entire universe.

While it is easy for most of us to extend gratitude to the first two or three circles, it is a challenge to go beyond. This is simply because it is easier for us to relate to people that we deal with regularly. Moving beyond these close circles involves stepping out of our comfort zone. For instance, it might not occur to us generally to be thankful to policemen, unless we find ourselves in a situation involving them.

As of today, where do you stand on the gratosphere scale? Does your gratitude extend beyond your own family and friends to include the doorman of your favorite restaurant or the sweeper who ensures that your street is tidy? Or do you find it easy to be grateful to strangers but not to your own immediate family?

Tied closely to this is the concept of the thankometer. While gratosphere is the length to which gratitude extends, thankometer is the depth. It is the frequency, span and intensity to which gratitude is felt and expressed. It is a way of measuring thankfulness by becoming more aware of the level and intensity of your gratitude. An extreme that the pendulum can swing towards, is the attitude that you are already thankful for everything, that there is nothing more left to be thankful for. That idea can be limiting - research too suggests that when you are looking for things to be grateful for, even if you don't exactly know what they might be, you can't help but feel good about yourself.

The quality of our life depends on our focus, attention and what we spend time on. Do you want to invest energy in being thankful or into complaining, cribbing and cursing? This decision impacts how the brain gets rewired. Expanding the circle of gratitude begins with us, one step at a time.

360 degrees gratitude encourages us to increase the span to include everyone in our sphere at home, office, the community and even random strangers as well as people we may never meet. Can we increase the intensity of our gratitude expression and the frequency as well? Can we make it specific instead of generic and include more number of people.

Practice: Gratitude Zones

Make a Gratitude Wall. Use stickers, pin boards, reminders, danglers, posters etc. besides sticky notes to express gratitude to someone.

String up celebration balloons around the gratitude zone.

Hang a gratefulness bell in the zone that people can ring every time they feel gratitude.

Make a 'Complaint Free Area' - a designated zone in your office or home and tag it as no complaint space. Allow people to express without complaining. Doing it for the first time needs some investment of time and materials. You will find yourself frequently spending time in these areas during the day to top up your happiness. Feel energized during the day as you spend time in such zones.

THANKOMETER
OF
LIFE

WHAT IS YOUR
LEVEL OF THANKFULNESS?

Universe	☐
Earth	☐
Living things	☐
Community	☐
Office	☐
Family	☐
Individual	☐

Span	:
Intensity	:
Density	:
Specificity	:
Frequency	:

(Low/Medium/High)

A gratefully disposed person would experience gratitude more intensely than someone less grateful, they would feel grateful more often, and do so for a relatively minor reason, they would have more sources of gratitude at any point, and would feel gratitude to a larger number of people per positive outcome than someone else. (Wood, Maltby, Stewart & Joseph, 2008b).

37

6

GRATITUDE SANS EXPECTATIONS

*Before you feel sorry for what is still lacking, invite
your-self to be thankful for what is already fulfilled.*

On one of my birthdays, a few years ago, I decided that instead of
people wishing me on my Facebook wall, I would ask them to
contribute to my charity for women entrepreneurs and children,
which I would accept as my birthday greetings. About 150 people
contributed and I ended up giving the money for the education
of a child who used to run a tea shop across the road from my
office and to a person who had lost his legs in a train accident. I
wasn't sure at the time of collecting the money about whether I
was doing it because it gave me happiness - and perhaps an ego
boost - or I was doing it as an altruistic selfless gesture.

Either way, I was thankful that the donation helped someone in
need. It got me thinking about what my true nature was - giving,
receiving or matching. I realized that I used to consider receiving
favors and emotional support as a burden and thought of it as
something to be returned. At work, I was always oriented
towards matching whatever I received but with close family and
friends I figured my proclivity was to give rather than receive.

Some of us are very afraid of giving. I've seen people afraid of giving gratitude for the fear that their blessings would be taken away, so they wouldn't speak about their good fortune or blessings, knocking wood to scare away the evil spirit. I've seen people afraid of receiving because when the time came they couldn't return it or as they said it is too big a favor and beyond their capability to give back or reciprocate ever. Some people are obsessed with matching in precise equal measures whatever they receive or give.

Since the giving, receiving and matching varies with circumstances, it is difficult to know the appropriateness in each situation without going through the burden of guilt, obligation or insecurity.

The true balance is in being grateful in all three situations. Givers are the people who tend to always fulfill other people's wants and needs. They are always ready to give everything that others ask for, sometimes at the cost of their own well-being. It leads to people manipulating them and their generosity is easily taken for granted, eventually burning them out.

Receivers only believe in taking from other people and tend to live life with the notion that the world owes them. Matchers, instead, try to match or coordinate their receiving and giving. They believe in giving when it's time to give and don't back off when it's time to receive. But sometimes they seem so caught up with the drama of the debit and credit that they tend to miss the larger picture.

The balance here is about giving and receiving with joy. Being equally grateful to all opportunities for giving and receiving brings us into that state of balance and bliss. Can we get ourselves in the positive cycle: giving leads to happiness and happiness promotes giving.

Our self expression is our way of giving to this world the best of our talents, gifts and blessings. This self expression is also a form of gratitude; it is an acknowledgement of that which we are blessed with.

Sometimes people take something from us and leave. We are used to calling such people ungrateful. To me the word ingratitude or ungrateful doesn't make sense as it reduces gratitude to a transactional level of indebtedness. Sometimes, what was given might have rippled elsewhere to affect others and not returned to us in this time and space.

Instead of keeping a stock and making a list of all the things that have taken something and left how about creating lists of all the people and things you are grateful for? Check your gratitude inventory with this exercise.

Practice: Gratitude Inventory

Make a master list of things that you are grateful for - people, places, situations, life events, challenges, gifts and talents - and express gratitude towards them. Then, fill out details in each category. You can also come up with categories that you can add to the master list.

This exercise brings back to awareness blessings that you may have forgotten about and gives you a chance be grateful to them. Make your list as exhaustive and comprehensive as possible. Use the gratitude inventory of lists as a reminder whenever your focus shifts towards what you do not have.

Relish the ripple effect of positive feelings that will reach your heart.

STOCKING
UP
GRATITUDE

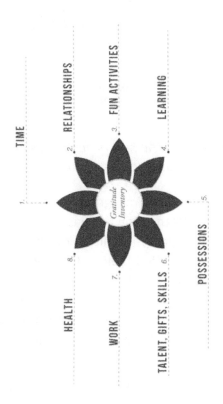

You can use this page to write down the list.
of things that you are Grateful for.

7

THE FOREST OF THANKFULNESS

Seeding gratitude in the hearts and minds of individuals, organizations and communities leads to forests of thankfulness

I was greatly impacted by my grandmother's death since we shared a close bond. Witnessing her passing away peacefully was the recognition of my own mortality. How much I had taken life for granted and how entitled I felt to the love, health, happiness and material comforts around me. Along with our DNA, we also pass on the qualities we are blessed with. She left in my heart the vibration of gratitude which she embodied throughout her life. I now channel it to the world through the Mission Billion Thanks initiative.

The easiest way to teach gratitude is by being so. What we demonstrate through our words, actions and presence is what people soak up as our energy, mirroring it back at us. One of the best relationship building tools is to say "thank you" and show appreciation all the time. A child may not express being grateful, but parents can lead the way by showing appreciation for small acts of kindness.

I went through a phase of taking up several psychometric assessments to know myself better. They could tell me my likes and preferences, certain characteristics and biases. The self-help books helped me become more aware. More than books, instructions, teachers, it's the practicing that helped me the most. I teach as a gratitude coach what I need to learn the most. When we talk about practicing the art of gratitude, we must know that gratitude is something that can be forced initially till we inculcate it fully into our being. When we expand our own gratitude consciousness, those around us and the world automatically absorbs and mirrors our energy and vibration.

Be it! When we are exercising the muscles of gratitude, we must be it, enjoy it, cherish it, value it, and reciprocate it in our own natural way. The practices in this book are all seeds of gratitude. When one starts applying a tiny and simple five-minute step coupled with nurturing, daily care, and attention, it can turn into a habit. Twenty one days of taking any of the exercises and applying them to any area of life can help in facing life's challenges.

The ability to bounce back from adverse circumstances can come from getting gratitude into our being. We all have had troubles and loss in our lives. While no one wishes for these kinds of challenges, we can be genuinely grateful for our capacity to gather the courage and resilience to carry on. Perhaps our most heroic act in the face of hardship is simply allowing our hearts to break and then transforming that pain into compassion, healing, and service.

The quality of death is something that I once discussed at an event called death cafe where groups meet up to discuss how they would like to leave this world. My sharing was, 'Even as my health fails me instead of being connected to endless tubes in a hospital room trying to extract the last bit of my life, I would like to leave this world with friends and loved ones around me, breathing gratefully till the end'.

Wanting to leave a legacy to contribute to this world and to leave our footprints on the sands of time is something that we all aspire for. But can we maximize the quality of our life and death with gratitude and plant the seed of gratitude in as many minds as possible?

Gratitude for past lessons, challenges and growth, gratitude for the present and gratitude for future goals, dreams and aspirations is the mantra that has given meaning and purpose to my life.

The ecosystem of friends, community (the sangha) that we give our time, attention and effort to; can support us on our path to grateful living.

Practice: Life as a Gratitude Festival

If we pause to look, there is a lot around us to appreciate.

When we create a festival of gratitude around us, in every moment, we create an atmosphere within and around us for celebration and appreciation.

Celebrate each day as a thanksgiving day by wishing well, appreciating, pampering ourselves and others, by creating a festive environment of grateful living around us.

Create occasions and opportunities for people to be more grateful. Encourage yourself/others around you to take up different gratitude challenges.

Organize retreats on weekends, vacations and community gatherings around the theme of gratitude.

HEALTHY
THANKFUL
BODY

GRATITUDE improves *well being* **10%** *by which is same impact as earning twice*

GRATITUDE JOURNAL *induces* **RELAXATION RESPONSE** *resulting in improved mood, relaxed muscles, lower blood pressure and heart rate*

GRATITUDE impacts **DEPRESSION** *Practicing Gratitude makes you feel less anxious*

GRATITUDE improves **IMMUNE FUNCTION** *Gratitude increases optimism and thereby our immune system*

GRATITUDE FOR YOUR HEALTH

GRATITUDE is **HAPPINESS** *Recognized after effect to be caused by the kindness of others*

GRATITUDE improves *resilience* **STRESS** *to and makes you more likely to offer support to others*

GRATITUDE improves **SLEEP** *Quality Duration* *Gratitude decreases time to fall asleep*

People practicing GRATITUDE **EXERCISE** **40** *mins on an average*

Keeping your body healthy is an expression of gratitude to the cosmos.

45

PART 2 : AWARENESS
THINKING

Dr. Big Head

THE RESILIENCE
OF A GRATEFUL WARRIOR

Chapters

Detox from Negativity

Power Drive of Gratitude

Trying but Failing

Greet-itude to Great-itude

Manifesting - Being a Channel of Blessing

Future Perfect Gratitude

Grateful Contentment with Joyful Improvement

THE RESILIENCE
OF A GRATEFUL WARRIOR

Practices

Grateful Forgiveness

Cursing to Cruising

But I am Grateful For

Stoned on Gratitude

Gratitude Vision Board & Reminders

Setting Grateful Intentions

Gratitude in the NOW

Dr. Big Head

8

DETOX FROM NEGATIVITY

*Gratitude cleanses your heart and mind of negativity,
expectations, worries and grudges.*

I used to pride myself on being a positive person but was surprised to note just how much my mind was tuned to pessimism, worry and negativity. At a joyshop conducted by my teacher Nithya Shanti, I was introduced to the practice of saying "Cancel Cancel Cancel" whenever I had a negative thought. It helped me to push negative thoughts away, bringing me back to the present moment. I used to practice looking in the mirror every time I washed my face or shaved, repeating that I am always grateful for everything, even something as small as receiving water in my tap.

Often, when we ask someone to not do something, just the usage of the word or sentence starting with 'don't' makes the brain imagine the thing to negate it as the brain doesn't understand how not to do something without creating an image of how to do it. Conditioning the mind to focus more on the positives than worry about the negatives can help to a large extent. Replace the word 'don't' with what you want more of.

The shift from victimhood to warrior hood (taking charge of a situation) is easier said than done, but not impossible. Pastor Will Bowen suggests that 21 days without complaining can help you get rid of the habit, bringing about a significant shift. This practice is something that I recommend in Chapter 22. Instead of blaming others, gratitude gives us a chance to find that which is worthy of appreciation in others and take complete responsibility for our actions and consequences of our choices.

Staying in the present moment and being mindfully engaged with what you are doing can indeed go a long way in discouraging feelings of anxiety and insecurity. Another good habit to adopt is the "not-my-monkey, not-my-circus" habit. The moment you become aware of being pulled into negativity coming from outside, simply remind yourself that whatever is the issue, it is their problem not yours, and gently disengage yourself from it.

Gratitude is the delicious loop of positivity that detoxes us from the vicious circle of negativity. Just these five words – "gratitude triggers positive feedback loops" - are the reason why gratitude is such a powerful antidote to worries, stress and negativity. It takes a few weeks of continuous practice for the larger benefits to appear since cultivating gratitude is a skill. After a week or two of practice, you can self-generate feelings of gratitude and happiness at will. Focusing on the task at hand helps release us from the loop of negativity. Doing this encourages us to stay in the present moment and overwrite anxiety and insecurities. As the famous stoic thinker Seneca once remarked, "True happiness is to enjoy the present, without anxious dependence upon the future."

When you cannot stop thinking and are feeling negative, it is often advisable to take the time to observe your feelings before you choose your reactions. This helps us respond to something more mindfully. Try and identify if negativity is a symptom of your stress. Our sources of stress can be people, circumstances, situations and our own thoughts about them. In such a situation, forgiving them and being grateful to them for our life lessons and growth is vital. Forgiveness and gratitude can be your 'sword and shield'.

Cancel, Cancel, Cancel: Whenever we get a negative thought, a treble recitation of the word cancel can make you aware and disrupt that thought.

Sometimes our negativity can be born out of our inability to forgive ourselves and others. Practices of grateful forgiveness are an excellent way of connecting back to our wholesome nature.

Practice: Grateful Forgiveness

Ho'oponopono, is a Hawaiian practice of forgiveness and reconciliation. Forgive and reconcile to move on in life. It is believed that there is nothing like 'out there' outside of you. Everything that is out there is within you. By healing yourself, you heal the people/environment around you. The four steps followed in this method are, Repentance, Forgiveness, Gratitude and Love.

Say the four simple yet powerful statements - "I am sorry, please forgive me, Thank you, I love you".

The Marwaris and Jains of my clan have a similar practice of saying Micchami Dukkadam to self and others, which is a way of saying: if through my words or deeds, intentionally or unintentionally, I have hurt you, I seek your forgiveness. This helps us connect back to our purity and wholeness.

PRAYER
OF
RECONCILIATION

ACCEPTANCE
Ms. WONDER

We are born into wholeness and purity. As we become older, we sometimes go out of sync with our wholeness. In such times, the Ho'oponopono is a Hawaiian practice of forgiveness and reconciliation. With these four sentences, we move from repentance to forgiveness to gratitude and love.

51

9

POWER DRIVEOF GRATITUDE

Life's journey gives better mileage
when you are tankful with gratitude.

While studying Computer Science at the Wright State University in Dayton, Ohio, I had an accident on the national highway on a rainy day. My car skid and just stopped short of going under a giant truck. The airbag burst in my face and the cops feared that I had broken my neck. Fortunately, I had only minor bruises despite the car being mangled completely. I was grateful to have survived and went on to buy my next car, but the accident left me deeply scarred. I also ended up with a fresh view towards driving and how we are when driving.

Driving gives us deep insight into our deservability, entitlement, desires, wants, expectations from others, control, faith, decision making etc.

For me and many others, driving is an exercise in noticing other people's attitudes, temperaments, following of rules, the state of roads, government and responsibility etc. Years later, based on these experiences where a lot of my friends were used to cursing, cribbing, and complaining when driving, I chanced upon a gratitude exercise that i call 'from cursing to cruising' when driving. Gratitude gets us to focus on the fact that there is a road and there are paths, signboards, vehicles. If we can focus on what's right, then we can have a more pleasurable ride.

On the road of life and the meandering path of our relationships, there are dead ends, wrong turns, U-turns. Gratitude positioning system is a GPS for navigation that cautions us about routes full of hurdles and how we can joyfully reach our destination by calibrating our journey. This guidance can help us navigate through the complex and complicated lessons that people and life teaches us.

It helps us wake up to our personal power and potential, rather than handing over life's controls in other people's hands. When we lose touch with ourselves and others' priorities take precedence over our own, we tend to be lost in the confusing by-lanes and shortcuts of burdensome responsibility and obligation. Gratitude for our priorities and for others gives us the balance required to take the long-distance journey of life.

When life brought me down through financial challenges, health issues and relationship breakdown, I learnt the meaning of humility and humbleness. When we are driven by egoistic power trip rather than gratitude, it can lead us to accidents, addictions and irreparable damage. Our anger and discomfort at what life throws at us as incoming traffic can make us fly into road rage; if we can respond with kindness and compassion at other people's needs and priorities then life can be on cruise control. Instead of cursing and showing the middle finger to all that triggers us, if we can do an ok, a thumbs-up, a wave of acknowledgement to soften our heart, we can be on a more conscious path of cruising with gratitude.

The journey of life is filled with sights and sounds, fellow travelers that come and go, of meeting and parting, of desire and repulsion. Only with thankfulness can you enjoy the bumps and the smooth stretches. Gratitude steers us on the path of enjoying what's in our control, joyfully doing what we can influence and letting go peacefully of what's not in our control.

In life, there is no destination, only the journey. In our quest for seeking and trying to find our reason for being here on earth, we need to ask ourselves: What are we driven by? Grateful self-expression or complaining, cursing, and cribbing.

The gratitude drive of thanking everything on your path can help you cruise rather than curse. Practice it the next time you go on a drive.

Practice: Cursing to Cruising

Meet the chaotic traffic head on so that you start your day on a positive note. Make driving more productive and joyful.

Every time you get behind the wheel, do not slip into complaining, cribbing and cursing.

Can we shift our mind's gear to reverse and be more Grateful about everything?

May be just the fact that we have roads to drive on, the rules to follow and prevent accidents and most people following them. The idea is to find enough things to actually appreciate.

While waiting at the signal, can we find things to admire, appreciate and be glad for? There are interesting sights around you like funny advertisements, a tiny patch of green in the midst of a concrete jungle or anything that can make you smile.

FROM
CURSING TO
CRUISING

Were you *kind* today?

In my journey of life, am I driven by compassion, kindness, and grace?
Did I praise, did I acknowledge someone?
Did I smile? Did I help when I could?
Did I empathise? Were my words soft?

10

TRYING BUT FAILING

*Before actual failure happens, it takes
place first in our minds and words.*

My mathematics teacher in high school had a rather imposing personality with a thick moustache and a heavy voice, which somehow always had us kids terrorized. He would insist on every student keeping a diary to write everything that he taught us in class. We would listen to him with rapt attention; make notes and obediently journal all that which was our learning for that day. This was my first attempt at writing a journal and it eventually turned into the habit of writing a personal diary that in turn led me to maintain a digital gratitude journal. He taught us the 'x but y' equation which essentially means when you put a 'but' between x and y, the x statement is untrue and only y is true.

This is equally applicable to how we think. When we make an x BUT y statement, we mean statement x is a lesser truth than statement y. For example, "I want to quit smoking, but from tomorrow" or "I am good but I'm always lazy." Or "Your show was very well received but the ratings could be better." Read each sentence again carefully and notice what sticks to your mind. Even though I have not used a single negative word, the sentence is not a positive one, the 'but' being the operative word. Our brain is quick to catch it. Now notice how many times you use the word but in your conversations and what impact it can have on people.

We sometimes use 'but' to refute the reality of our lives. We make a positive statement and reduce or negate its meaning by interjecting it with 'but'. While we use it for communication with others extensively, we use it to communicate with ourselves too.

There was a big positive impact on my gratitude mindset when I started measuring the number of times I was saying 'but' per day and eventually replacing it with 'and'. This also helps weed out the negative messages going into your sub-conscious, the 'and' making it inherently positive. You enter an agreement mind frame because 'and' is not used to disagree, but to add something extra. With an 'and', both parts are equally emphasized. You are moving out of an 'argument frame' and entering an 'agreement frame'. This infuses a whole lot of positivity if done daily. Replacing 'but' with 'and' gets me into a more agreeable frame of mind, which in turn helps me deal with any situation far more effectively.

'Try' is no different. When a colleague invites you to a house-warming party, the easiest way to wriggle out of it is to say "I will try to come" because it gives you an excuse to fall back upon. If you don't go, "trying" is an excuse mechanism for when we are not sure. Trying is giving the brain and ourselves permission to fail while doing gives us the power to put in our best.

When you say, "I will try going to the gym twice a week", you are giving your subconscious a message that there are no consequences of failing to do it. Instead if you say "I will go to the gym thrice a week" - you remain firm with your intention with no room for complacency - because you omitted the word "try".

In gratitude practices too we can either try or do. If we use sentences like "I am very grateful to my parents but I don't express it often" or "I am grateful to everything but I just don't like being appreciated for anything", then we know where our gratitude practices end up.

However, there are times when 'but' is very useful. When we are overwhelmed with challenges or difficult situations, the phrase "but I'm grateful for" can help us find that tiny streak of positivity to hold on to.

Practice: But I am grateful for

'But I'm grateful for' is a way of finding that proverbial silver lining in dark clouds. When in adversity, if we say 'but I'm grateful for...' we learn to focus on what we do have.

When I was in dire financial adversity, I remember reminding myself again and again, "I may not have money but I'm grateful to be working."

This shift in our world view involves looking at a negative situation and finding something in it to be grateful for. In life's major challenges and problems, can we think of something in this moment, however small, that is positive and helpful? It can help us find light and direction, an anchor when caught in a raging storm.

REDUCE
THE SIZE OF
YOUR BUT

DO, OR DO NOT...
THERE IS NO TRY

AWARENESS
Dr. Big Head

YES OR NO...
THERE ARE NO IFS AND BUTS

*'But' is a word that causes us to be in a frame of disagreement,
replacing it with 'and' moves us towards agreeing with reality.
Arguing with reality causes suffering. Getting into a mode of 'and'
instead of 'but' helps us co-create reality with the universe.*

Grateful Pause

Hey I'm Prashant Jain here, the author of the book.

Hope you feel connected so far, finding it useful and fun. If you are, please do me a favour, use the following link to rate the book and write a review. My ambitious goal for this book is to be considered as a" Goto book of gratitude practices" and one way to ensure it is by getting some Amazon reviews and love on the following link

https://www.amazon.in/dp/8192349551/

P.S : you can interact with me on my website
www.prashantjain.in or email me contact@prashantjain.in

Gift from Author

Download free printable Gratitude Workbook
http://www.vitamingratitude.com

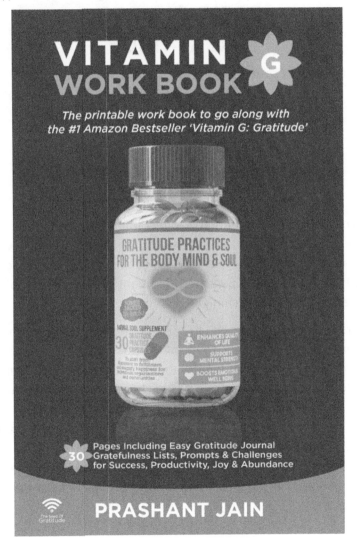

11

GREET-ITUDE TO GREAT-ITUDE

Greet-itude is welcoming everything - both challenges and blessings with equal acceptance.

For the longest time, I had anger management issues. The slightest provocation would set me off. All life's challenges would find a way to distract me from a path of being calm and peaceful. Whatever I resisted, it persisted adamantly. I was on a path of self-healing and not reaching anywhere significant.

Under test conditions, as in during workshops and in the presence of a supportive community, I was able to handle myself but the same patterns of anger would repeat when I get back to real life situations. I was afraid of my challenges, growing anxious at the thought of facing them, wanting only certainty, comfort, status quo and stability. This fear of challenges of anger management in emotional, financial and health areas made me a constant worrier. I noticed that besides my avoidance strategy, other people had different ways of handling challenges and adversities.

In childhood some of us are scared of exams even though we know that the test is required to progress to the next level. Pain in any area of life is a sign that life wants us to focus on that part. If our adversities are here to teach us a lesson, shouldn't we be prepared for the bad times during our good times by exercising the muscle of gratitude? We exercise so that we can break down the fat and create muscle, by breaking down the old pattern and rebuilding it to create new. For this we have to push the boundaries of our status quo and comfort zone.

The perennial "victim worrier" looks at challenges with fear and insecurity. The "grateful warrior" has an attitude of positivity, welcoming challenges as stepping stones for growth, expanding wisdom, and greater self-awareness. I discovered the attitude of "greet-itude", which is to welcome all challenges and say "bring it on". This technique helped me develop a sense of positivity. Welcoming everything in life is an art that comes with practice. There is no manual in the world to teach us how we can greet life. It is born out of acceptance and joyful practice of applying ourselves every day.

We have a choice to approach life with fear, worry and anxiety or with curiosity, wonderment and gratitude. If we want to accept the challenge - we have to face it and take it on like a warrior. Being passionate and intense about gratitude helps us to approach everything with confidence in one self. Rather than resisting a challenge, you will find yourself curious about what is it here to teach and how it will contribute to your growth. Avoiding and resisting a challenge is a sign of stagnation setting into your life. I discovered this during my struggles and being in the same stagnant place of health, wealth, and spirit for almost four years.

Namaste - a word originating from the beautiful and ancient language of Sanskrit, is the Indian way of greeting with folded hands that gratefully says – "the highest in me bows to the highest in you". The term contains, in its ancient roots, an essence that can be life-changing. This is a way of acknowledging the highest potential in us and in others.

Have you said Namaste to your challenges, to face them and conquer your fears like a warrior?

It is a personal choice to adopt the attitude of taking up new challenges and greet life in a completely different way. Approaching everything, including death, with a greeting of thankfulness, can indeed ensure a far elevated quality of life.

In our times of challenges, we need something to remind us of all the things we are grateful for. To face challenges why not be high on bliss and stoned on gratitude?

Practice: Stoned On Gratitude

Keep a small pebble or stone as a touch-and-feel anchor for reminding you of what you might be grateful for in the moment. Keep this stone with you always or you can leave it at a place where you will see it often at home or work. In challenging times, this stone can remind you of things to be grateful for in your life.

Any smooth round stone that fits in your purse or wallet will do. Transfer all your feelings of gratitude to it. Hold it at regular intervals as a reminder.

TEST
OF
GRATITUDE

1.	Gratitude comes from looking at how much better off you are than others	☐ True	☐ False
2.	You have to be grateful all the time to alter neural pathways	☐ True	☐ False
3.	Grateful people are just as materialistic as ungrateful people	☐ True	☐ False
4.	Being grateful can help you have fewer bodily aches and pains	☐ True	☐ False
5.	Keeping a gratitude journal will decrease depression and make you more optimistic in general	☐ True	☐ False
6.	Gratitude helps you sleep better and longer	☐ True	☐ False
7.	Gratitude is a great motivation	☐ True	☐ False
8.	It doesn't matter what we are grateful for, as long as we thank, our brains will benefit	☐ True	☐ False
9.	The best antidote against a sarcastic or crude tongue is gratitude	☐ True	☐ False
10.	It isn't important who or what you thank, as long as you practice gratitude	☐ True	☐ False

Mark True or False in above sentences and check results in the following chapter practice.

12

MANIFESTING AND BEING A CHANNEL OF BLESSINGS

*The universe can't be cajoled or seduced especially by
an advance payment of gratitude with expectation*

About a decade ago, I had made a goal sheet and vision board of the things I wanted at that time. Over the next five years, I forgot about it. One day I happened upon them and realized that I had surpassed all of my goals three years before the expected time. Such was my focus and dedication towards what I wanted that I had attracted it almost effortlessly.

Having trained thousands of sales people over 20 years of my work as an entrepreneur, I would always ask my team members to keep a goal sheet written in bold with a clear intention to help them remain focused on targets and goals.

Thoughts have great energy. When we are grateful we count our blessings and attract more of it. When we focus on our limitations and 'bad luck' we attract those experiences instead. Our thoughts create our reality and what we focus on expands. As human beings, we have a limited amount of attention for all the stuff going on around us. Therefore, we are always choosing what we pay attention to. Confirmation bias is the human mind's tendency to notice and pay more attention to things that match its pre-existing beliefs. It does this for the simple reason that it is biologically economical and efficient.

We can become good manifestors with focused thought, attention and inspired action. We are manifesting all the time, whether we are aware of it or not. With focused thought, attention and inspired action you consciously manifest what you want. But I have noticed that quite often our expression of gratitude is need based. We thank the universe because we got something from it, or we're expecting something.

We need to be thankful for things we receive and those we are yet to receive. Often, we want things not because we love them but because we love the idea of the feeling it might give us once we own that thing. For instance, we obsess about a new car. We might not love the car itself but are completely taken in by the feeling of owning and driving that vehicle. We might sometimes not really need the thing, just the feeling of owning it is what we are aiming at. Asking for what you want is good, but it makes all the difference to be clear about why we want what we want. What is it that you already have that can make you feel content and complete in this moment?

Most of us tend to focus on what hasn't happened, what didn't meet our expectations, and the dissatisfactions in life rather than noticing what we already have and what else can we open ourselves to receive. Our attitude is about being grateful for something in favor of something, to treat gratitude as a payment for something that we're expecting in future. The idea that we are a channel of blessing for others means that we are allowing good positive things to flow through us without an expectation of the result. The tree doesn't care who enjoys its shade or fruit or that it has to pay it back to the original planter and nurturer. It simply lives its full potential.

As creators and manifestors of our lives, we can become a channel of blessing for others in manifesting their dreams, aspirations and goals. By becoming the device of their blessings, we experience the shift of going from "for me" to "through me" for the greater good of others and the entire world. A vision board and Reminders are an excellent way of keeping your goals before your eyes and in your mind.

Practice: Gratitude Vision Board and Reminders

Make a collage with pictures from magazines, photographs or drawings etc. and create a vision board of all things you are grateful for, including your aspirations and goals. You can also make a digital wallpaper collage of your past and present achievements besides future goals. Set focus and intention on being thankful as if these dreams from the vision board have already come true and manifested.

Set a daily or weekly reminder on your phone to help you be regular with your gratitude practices. Set up a roadmap to practice gratitude with visual cues like Gratitude key chains, posters, fridge magnets. Visual cues stimulate your brain and help you keep up the spirits.

LAW
OF
FOCUS

*'What you focus on expands.
Are you focussing on your problems or your blessings?'*

13

FUTURE PERFECT GRATITUDE

True transformation begins on the inside. The outside world is only a reflection.

During my electronics engineering days, I would make small gadgets and sell them to friends. This was my first go at entrepreneurship. Three years later, during my Master's in the US, I was already web designing. A few years later, in 1997, I was running one of the first e-commerce ventures in India. I then ventured into multiple businesses including web services, hosting, data centers, corporate gifting and now I focus on my work on gratitude. In all my choices, the aspirations had come from the clarity of being grateful for what I had and yet simultaneously making efforts towards growing. When we balance our aspirations for the future in the grounding of the present, we grow a forest of thankfulness.

Without dreams and goals, we cannot grow. Being grateful for our dreams and aspirations, gives us the impetus required to grow instead of only counting our blessings. When we are grateful for what we are anticipating in the future, it changes our perception, taking the form of trust and getting us into the vibration of receiving.

Complacency and laziness are the hallmarks of not being in gratitude as gratitude leads us to action, not stagnancy. Gratitude heals our relationship with time by getting us to make sense of our past through thankfulness for the lessons learnt from previous choices. Gratitude also enables us to focus on what's important and not just on what is urgent.

Being in a state of gratitude can lead to increased determination, energy and enthusiasm to achieve your dreams and goals. It has been proved that negativity inhibits our ability to think clearly and we become blind to opportunities. On the other hand, gratitude leads us to be optimistic and positive. Optimism and positivity are traits that help us achieve and have what we want. Leaving things to the universe and god without doing your bit is being lazy and complacent. The drop in the ocean also contributes to the ocean just as the ocean is only a sum total of the drops. To make our dreams and aspirations come true and to manifest them, we have to co-create them with the universe.

Ultimately, the statement that 'if you just think about what you want, it will come to you' - when taken to its logical extreme, it might encourage one to always be wanting something, to never be content, and this can make us less happy in the long run. Don't wish for good rewards, wish for good problems. Gratitude keeps us away from delusional positivity and encourages us to look at problems as opportunities. Our intent can be for the future but our attention must be in the present.

As Humans have freewill we know, interpretations of Inshallah, Amen, Thatatsu are all in the meaning of 'along with the will of god.' Our life is a co-creation along with the universe.

Humans are designed for aspiring more and more. We are encouraged not to rest on our laurels but constantly strive for more, better and bigger.

Setting an intention, according to Buddhist teachings, is quite different from goal setting. It's not oriented toward a future outcome. Instead, it is a path or practice that is focused on how you are 'being' in the present moment. Your attention is on the ever-present now in the constantly changing flow of life.

This attitude helps us achieve more but deprives us of living in the moment. Focusing on your intentions does not mean you give up your goals or desire for achievement. By balancing between goals and intentions, you enjoy the journey as much as the destination.

Practice: Setting Grateful Intentions

Allowing intentions to guide our moment to moment focus means living our values and what matters most to us. Write a sentence or a word of your intention as a reminder. The visual stimulus will reinforce the commitment to live by that intention.

Use power words for your intentions like Calm, Peace, Harmony, Balance, Prosperity, Presence, Smile, Joy and so on. Use words that will bring about a change in whatever challenge you are dealing with.

Allow yourself to fully live and be the word or sentence chosen. Keep an open mind about how this practice will play out as it has tremendous potential and possibilities.

THE FUTURE
OF
GRATITUDE

Taking for granted

Entitlement

Envy

Scarcity

Cursing

Cribbing

Complaining

Negativity

THE GRATEFUL PLANET

When we rise above complaining, cribbing, cursing, whining we create an atmosphere through the 6As to reach a state of grateful living.

On the wings of thankfulness and gratitude, we can raise the consciousness of this planet.

73

14

FROM CONTENTMENT TO JOYFUL IMPROVEMENT

Gratitude doesn't bypass reality;
it makes us focus on inspired action.

About six years ago, with one of the cloud computing businesses we started online; I had set a revenue goal of one billion rupees for that financial year. I was pushing my sales teams hard and we were working in an ambience of frustration and anxiety with all of us being stressed out to meet our deadline. We had exhausted ourselves emotionally and mentally and a few of my team members even had severe health breakdowns given the high stress. We had challenged ourselves to go way beyond the limitations and boundaries of the marketplace in which we were operating. Our goals were - in management parlance S.M.A.R.T (Specific, Measurable, Achievable, Relevant and Time bound) - yet that year we struggled without success. I became too closely identified with the one-billion target and was utterly heartbroken when we didn't make it. Years of stagnancy and laziness during my depression phase had slowed me down and this aspiration was too much of challenge. An insight I had in the midst of all the emotions was that I could enable my growth by supporting myself through gratitude and challenging myself enough such that I would also achieve my dreams.

From a place of fear we can drive ourselves to frustration and anxiety or we can be inspired, looking for 'joyful' improvement zooming from the ground reality of grateful contentment. My teacher Nithya Shanti's quote of "everything is perfect and joyfully improving" is a mantra that helps me retain my balance at turbulent times. I have found goals - smart or otherwise - to be future focused and nowadays I set being level intentions so that I can act from that in every moment. Finding the balance is the key.

Gratitude is essential to combat our instinctive fear-based survivalist approach. We focus on problems because our amygdala, the instinctive survival brain is focused on lack and scarcity. Whether it's a human being or organization, there's a constant quest for self-improvement and growth. Modern organizations are constantly planning for contingency more than they are planning for success. This is because our motivation during the evolution process was the fear of death, which has now morphed into fear of rejection or failure. When we look at problems without focusing on solutions, we will only create more problems.

Highly driven people sometimes mistake the attitude of gratitude for passive stagnancy. Gratitude, in fact, inspires everything else except stagnancy. Even with doing gratitude practices, our greatest growth is in finding the right balance of challenge and support. The trick to becoming an expert in this balancing act is to iterate enough number of times such that we find a flow that will give us the maximum results

The more thankful we are for what we have now, the quicker we can have that which we are looking for. No matter which stage you are at in your own life, you can enhance your circumstance significantly by simply concentrating on being appreciative all the time. Finding this right balance between challenging and supporting ourselves can be an everyday daunting task. Sometimes we get tied to our ideas of perfection, thereby losing sight of what can be done in the moment to strive forward. Whenever I find myself in the midst of things that I like or those that I don't, I hold the invitation in my heart: "how can I make this even better?"

Between the regrets of the past and the potential of the future lies the present moment of action which requires our best inspiration and motivation. Shouldn't we begin this action by patting ourselves on the back and being grateful for the NOW?

Practice: Gratitude in the NOW

Generally, we dream of big things like that ultimate relationship or dream home but life is composed of several small things too to be grateful for. What is it that you can be grateful for in this very moment? Take a moment and find something spontaneously and thank it.

The basic law is that whatever we focus on expands and whatever we resist persists. So, if we tunnel our focus on the lack of things in life, we will attract more lack. Focusing on expanding whatever is positive in this present moment may be just the fact that we are alive, breathing and reading, this can get us into a state of gratitude for the NOW.

GRATITUDE REMINDERS

Keep reminders around your house, office, car, devices, body to remind yourself to focus on living Gratefully.

Results of previous chapter practice

1, 2, 3 are False and the remaining are True

PART 3 : $\frac{\text{ⒶCCEPTANCE}}{\text{FEELING}}$

Ms. Wonder

DISCOVERING JOY &
INNER ABUNDANCE

Chapters

Undervalued & Unrecognised

Millennial Entitlement

Grief & Guilt

Postponed Happiness and Joy

Comparison and Envy

Selfie Esteem

Inner Abundance

DISCOVERING JOY & INNER ABUNDANCE

Practices

Self Love & 100% Responsibility

Practicing Poverty & Minimalism

G2G, from Sorry to Thank You

Gratitude Visits and Letters

Mudita, joy in another's joy

Grateful Self Acceptance

Magnifying Gratitude

Ms. Wonder

15

UNDERVALUED UNRECOGNIZED

*Feeling undervalued and unappreciated occurs
when self-love is the missing piece in the life puzzle.*

One of my friends, who had been a homemaker for fifteen years, recently shared with me how today she is a digital nomad, tech entrepreneur and author, writing her book in places like Bali and Ecuador. She spent most of her life feeling undervalued and unappreciated. While keeping house and taking care of her family was something she loved, she realized that her focus was never on herself. It wasn't the others but she who had undervalued herself, and finally after many years, decided to respect and honor her individuality. This is something that each one of us needs to do, starting with ourselves and our body itself.

It's easy to slip into the pit of feeling unappreciated and dejected with an attitude that we are giving far more than we can ever receive. How many times have you taken yourself and your body for granted, as against those times when you felt truly grateful for your body? We put our bodies through so much damage. There are times when we do not sleep enough, when we smoke and drink, when we eat unhealthy food or eat haphazardly. Our body tries so hard to cope with the abuse and yet we don't stop. Most people are not happy with the body they have and body shaming on social media only makes us hate our bodies even more.

When we do not have enough self-worth, we end up blaming others for not appreciating us. Such negativity, in turn, pulls us into a vicious circle. We experience low self-esteem and then try to compensate for it from the outside. Lack of appreciation then pulls us deeper into misery. When you turn inward though, gratitude can bring you back towards appreciating and valuing what you already have and it is then that you can show appreciation to others.

Creating a culture of appreciation for yourself and others can be highly beneficial not just for your emotional state but also your physical health. Each of us can have our own parameters of appreciating people around us. This will indeed create a whirlpool of appreciation and happiness, which has a direct impact on health and well-being.

Generally, by force of our social environment, we keep our circle very limited. It consists of our family, friends and maybe a few others. So, we end up drawing an extremely finite circle around us. This has a direct impact on our behavior. We are good at showing gratitude to our close ones but when it comes to dealing with the greater world or others outside that circle, we are not so open. The circle of gratitude should be big enough to encompass the entire world, eventually. Your goodness emanates and radiates from you, even if it is not noticed by the world around you. We do not need the idea of being valued or appreciated by others, as Marcus Aurelius writes in his book, The Meditations, "An emerald shines even if it is not spoken of".

A space where people routinely appreciate each other in small ways is bound to radiate more happiness.

Many times, we make choices without recognizing the consequences of our actions and give away the remote control of our lives to others. What we need really is endorsement, appreciation and acceptance from ourselves. Right now, put down this book and simply pat yourself on the back for having outdone the million sperms among which you emerged as an individual, got a name and identity and arrived this far.

Practice: Self Love and 100% Responsibility

Taking responsibility for our own happiness also means taking care of ourselves. Pamper yourself today in some way - gift yourself a little gift, a flower, or a massage, or any experience you enjoy. This is a way of directing gratitude towards self.

Deep breathing coupled with positive visualizations about the self are immensely powerful as well. We can keep reinforcing that we alone are responsible for making ourselves happy and repeating affirmations of self-love like "I choose to fully and completely love and accept myself."

While external factors may be influenced to a small extent, they are never in our complete control; however, our reactions and responses are. Gratitude teaches us to take 100% responsibility for ourselves, our decisions and our lives.

PROMPTS
FOR
SELF LOVE

Take an inventory in all the above areas that you are Grateful for.

16

MILLENNIAL ENTITLEMENT

*The quantity and quality of life are directly proportional
to the amount of thankfulness we live by.*

I was guiding a teenager with his school project. He was digitally quite clued in and constantly fiddling with his phone, spending most of his time in the virtual world. He yearned for Facebook likes more than human appreciation. His quest was to be famous on Instagram and have several virtual friends; he had no real friends at all. His world was all about hashtags and notifications.

My attempts to keep him away from the virtual world were only turning him more sullen. He could not relate to what he was doing when kept away from his gadgets. A few counseling sessions later, he came across as depressed and lonely with his only motive being recognized and celebrated in the virtual world. I convinced him to take a detox travel trip away from social media. We live in a world deeply addicted to our digital lives and our sense of self is very fragile.

Today's age is a culture of entitlement. Entitlement is an attitude wherein people believe that privileges are their right.

From small outbursts at restaurants for being served tea not piping hot to being uncaring and self-centered in relationships, a sense of entitlement is all pervading. Narcissism is at the very heart of this trait; the over exaggerated sense of self-importance. We need to question the view: does the world owe us a great life, loving caring parents, a great childhood and all the comforts? And if it does not happen, can we still be grateful?

When we were young it was kind of cute when we threw tantrums as toddlers. People would cuddle us, be amused by our behavior. Then our tears were mopped, our snotty little noses wiped. As we grow older, some of us learned to wait for our turn, be patient and show consideration for others. Some of us, however, didn't. We continue throwing tantrums, only in a more sophisticated way. We also continued to expect special treatment just because we're us and therefore we deserve it. Having a sense of entitlement is a skewed form of self-love that can harm others and us in the long term.

The millennium has brought us unprecedented progress. Survival got redefined with everything at our fingertips, thanks to technology. From knowledge to relationships, everything is currently available online - more so in an app and digital form. From learning to ski to making a bomb, all kinds of knowledge is available at the click of a button. Everything is instantly served - there's no gradual process here, only a demand for instant gratification. Technologically equipped, those of us living in the internet era have the ultimate power our ancestors would have considered a myth, legend or even sorcery. This itself can give us such a high sense of entitlement moving us away from gratitude.

Simon Sinek, who authored the bestseller 'Start with Why: How Great Leaders Inspire Everyone to Take Action', says that the dependence on technology leads to an increasing loss of meaningful relationships, with people turning to the virtual world rather than a real person for sharing their troubles.

Most of the time, entitlement is about the attitude "I need to be given what I want, regardless of everything else" and over personalizing this feeling. When we zoom out from this perspective with the idea that the world doesn't owe me anything, we may feel sudden emptiness but it will soon lead to a feeling of joy and lightness. Gratitude is the recognition that life owes me nothing and all the good I have is a gift.

Practice: Practicing Poverty & Minimalism

I have tried a few experiments of resetting my expectation from life based on the Seneca's idea of practicing poverty. Eat less, wear your worst clothes, and get away from the comfort of your home and bed. It's important to remember that this is an exercise and not a rhetorical device. He doesn't want us to "think about" misfortune, instead, live it to know what is taken for granted.

I practice this every year for a week at least and it has helped me become more sensitive and appreciative of life's blessings.

Minimalism helps us realize what is most important to us and what we value the most. Eliminating the excess and unimportant allows us to acknowledge all the wonderful things filling our life that we are grateful for. Minimalism is about reducing stuff to make room for more life.

MILLENIAL ENTITLEMENT MENTALITY

An attitude of entitlement is inversely related to one of gratitude

17

GRIEF AND GUILT

*The purpose of grief may be to teach us
deep acceptance of life with gratitude.*

India lost to Australia in the semi-finals of the 2015 ICC Cricket World Cup. In a roomful of friends, the first reaction to this loss was that of shock and disbelief - "this can't be happening to the Indian cricket team". Next came the sadness of "why us" which eventually turned to anger. I saw my friends oscillate between the phases of dismay / shock, sadness/disbelief and anger/ denial and then they vented their emotions on Facebook. The next day, these three phases transformed into bargaining of "if not this, the next world cup" and "let's appreciate the team we lost out to" etc. This bargaining eventually turned into an acceptance of it just being a game. It's a deeper sense of acceptance when we think: win or loss, it was fun to have witnessed a spectacular match!

Grief is a natural response to having lost someone or something we have held to be precious whether it's something as small as a cricket match or as huge an event as the loss of a loved one. The end of a relation, the death of someone close, the change of career or chronic health issues tend to initiate a cycle of grief that can last for days, months and sometimes even years. Sadness and loneliness is a vicious cycle triggered by life changing events that alter the chemistry of our brain. To rewire and find joy, we must understand the nature of grief and walk through its stages to find acceptance and gratitude.

Elisabeth Kubler-Ross, first proposed the five-stage grieving process in her book On Death and Dying. These stages are: denial – depression - anger - bargaining - acceptance, not necessarily in the same order. The first stage of grieving is denial as we are either unaware or refuse to accept that we are grieving. The second stage is anger where we watch the world go about its business, while perceiving that only we are suffering and ask repeatedly: WHY ME? There are some who get stuck in this stage life-long and end up becoming embittered and cynical.

Sadness is that feeling of intense emotions wringing you out and twisting you into a knot. At times, sadness can make you dysfunctional in your day to day life and you are unable to respond to overtures of help offered by well-wishers around. Next comes bargaining - you either bargain with your own self or with god. Sometimes people make promises to god, to their loved ones or to themselves in return for a situation not to occur again or for things to go back to how they were before the loss or change. The last stage is acceptance or acknowledgment. Only after this can you move on in life and be ready to face fresh battles.

Gratitude helps grieving souls transition from pause-life to pro-life. It builds resilience and develops emotional stamina. Grief also gives you deep appreciation of life - the loss of something valuable deepens the appreciation and awareness of it. After we experience loss, we tend to focus on what we no longer have. We focus our energy on that and miss out cherishing the wonderful things we still have. When we want what we don't have, we ignore what we do have. Being grateful for what remains after you have experienced a loss can be a powerful way to deal with and heal that loss.

Treasuring the times spent with a person in life is a better way of appreciating life than being endlessly bogged down by the vacuum left behind by that person's departure. Gratitude helps us rise above that loss, and perhaps most importantly, supports our move ahead and appreciate the abundance that surrounds us in the present.

Practice: G2G, from Sorry to Thank You

Can we move from guilt to gratitude and focus on the present without the shadow of past regrets? Guilt is being sorry for something and gratitude is being thankful. This shift involves finding the blessings and uniqueness of our circumstances rather than the faults and inadequacies.

The switch from sorry to thank you is a journey of going from guilt to gratitude. Even when accepting compliments, simply thank the person.

For example, if a colleague says "Great presentation", instead of putting yourself down by saying, "Did I? I was so nervous. "I'm glad it looked alright" say "Thank You. I'm happy it went well".

Instead of saying, "Sorry, I'm late" use "Thank you for your patience and waiting for me." This is another way of appreciating and acknowledging the quality in another person and enhancing it.

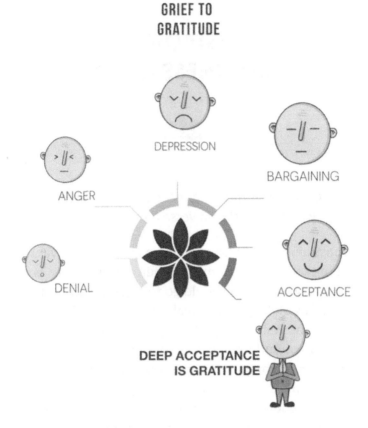

FROM GRIEF TO GRATITUDE

DEPRESSION

BARGAINING

ANGER

ACCEPTANCE

DENIAL

DEEP ACCEPTANCE IS GRATITUDE

The six stages, denial, anger, depression, bargaining, acceptance and finally deep acceptance leading to gratitude are a part of the framework that makes up our learning to live with loss. They are tools to help frame and identify what we may be feeling. But they are not stops on some linear timeline.

18

POSTPONED HAPPINESS & JOY

*Gratitude is the instant currency of now that
we repay to the universe for our existence.*

To not postpone happiness and live in the now is a valuable life lesson I picked up from my mother. After I was born, her constant worry was that I should go to a good school, after which her obsessions shifted to my higher education. Once I chose a career, she was waiting for me to get hitched so that she could finally be happy. And then, it was about the grandchildren... I call it the postponed cheque of happiness - happiness that you will cash in sometime in the future depending on an event which may or may not happen. Most of us believe that we will be thankful once we are happy. But it is rather the opposite. We will be happy when we are thankful. Gratitude is all about the present and finding happiness right now.

Instead of worrying about our past and fantasizing about the future, we must find ways to appreciate this moment and taking the joyous inspired effort required to move forward. Without actively engaging in this effort, our dreams remain mere fantasies.

Gratitude can be the fuel that pushes you forward towards your goals while keeping you firmly grounded in the present.

When people are happy, it is easy to be grateful and most of us tend to wait till we find that perfect moment of bliss and happiness. But happiness is ephemeral, sometimes we find it in power, in pleasures that money can buy, in our work and career, in fame and glory and sometimes even in our addictions. However, happiness is a choice we make, and we can make it without a reason or season. While happiness can be temporary and based on external pleasures, joy is an inner state of being that is not dependent on anything external. Gratitude is a powerful and beautiful path to joy.

An overtly materialistic lifestyle is about chasing happiness in consumerism, which comes and goes based on one's possessions. It has been scientifically proven that even when people win a lottery, after a few months they are back to feeling as they did before 'getting lucky' since their state of being hasn't changed. Researchers Marsha Richins and Scott Dawson developed the first scale to measure materialism - an indication to the extent to which people place material possessions at the centre of their lives. For more than two decades, studies have consistently found that people who score high on Dr. Richins and Dawson's scale scored lower on just about every major scale to measure happiness.

Instead of wanting what we do not have, gratitude helps us focus on what we do have and pursue our goals from that place of contentment and not incompleteness. Gratitude also teaches us not to take the positive things in our life for granted. Gratitude, though, is not about bypassing challenges or escapism guised in positivity. Instead, it means realizing the power you have to transform an obstacle into an opportunity.

Since gratitude can enable you to appreciate what you have and become less fixated on acquiring mindlessly, it will help build social bonds, strengthen existing relationships and nurture new ones. The vibration of gratitude is incompatible with negative emotions and with time, feelings like greed, jealousy and resentment start to diminish. Once you begin to feel it within you, you cannot help but spread it through your expression of who you are.

Staying in the present is cashing in on our present moment instead of postdating our cheque of happiness. You will be happy through giving undivided attention, mindful about every moment in life consistently.

Practice: Gratitude Visits and Letters

To amplify happiness, write a gratitude letter. Share it with someone who made your life happier by their presence. If possible, visit the person in question and share your appreciation with them.

You can also stick it at a place where it'll catch the eye of the recipient. Don't be shy about writing your honest feelings, or worried about how they will take it. If you have had a difficult relationship with them, focus on the good and positive parts of your connection.

If the person does not live in geographic proximity, instead of sending them an email, write a hand-written letter and take a picture and send it. Alternatively, you can also send an audio or video message.

KEY
TO
HAPPINESS

HAPPINESS → GRATITUDE ✗
GRATITUDE → HAPPINESS ✓

Money cannot buy us happiness.
Happiness is a consequence of Gratitude. Not the other way around.
Gratitude unlocks happiness, joy and abundance.

95

19

COMPARISON AND ENVY

*Gratitude is the instant currency of now that
we repay to the universe for our existence.*

At school, during sports activities, we would be asked to stand in a line in ascending order of height. There were only two boys shorter than I, which made me the third shortest boy in our class of about 50 students. Sometimes, I would feel bad comparing myself to the others and wished I was taller. Sometimes I would take solace in the fact that I was taller than at least two others in the class. As I grew older, I discovered my own uniqueness as a person. I started accepting my height. As time passed, I realized that comparison was something that kept leading me to unhappiness.

From the number of social media likes to the size of our material possessions, comparison is a constant in our lives. Even a digital Detox will help us overcome our ideas of comparison and envy if we stay focused on the self. Corporations compare numbers as a way of improvement. Competition is encouraged as a mantra for growth in our educational system and culture. Sometimes we end up going to the same restaurant or vacation and start comparing our last experience with the current one. Sometime in our relationships we compare how things were then and now.

We even end up comparing ourselves to how we used to be a source of inspiration and motivation.

The downside is that when you constantly compare your life with those of others, you always come up short. Over comparing causes envy - the feeling we have when we want to get something that someone else has and we can't be happy for them when they have it.

Comparison inevitably leads to envy for what others have which we don't, and often gives rise to jealousy - its meaner cousin that says 'I wish they didn't have it either'. Gratitude does the inverse where we remain thankful to what we have. Envy and jealousy are destructive while gratitude is an anti-dote to envy and jealousy.

Gratitude requires compassion for the self and tolerance for others and gives the ability to understand the value and abundance of our unique gifts. Gratitude is the affirmation of our enoughness, the enoughness of what we have, of who we are, of what we will become.

Jealousy and envy inevitably lead to wanting more and being more materialistic. Gratitude helps us positively focus on what we have, recognize our own unique gifts, blessings, and good fortune.

Tied closely to this is also the idea of forgiveness. Forgiveness is letting go of grudges, resentment, and bitterness that envy, anger, comparison, and victimhood breed. Forgiving ourselves and others can open the doors to gratitude.

Forgiveness can be a liberating feeling. It frees us from the negative attachment to a person who has hurt us. This unchains us from the cycle of negativity and opens our hearts to gratitude, happiness, and love once again. Anger and victimhood are born out of not acknowledging our blessings and being unable to find contentment with what we have.

We are unique and special, just like everyone else. We must comprehend that everybody is one of a kind as far as looks, deeds, accomplishments, abilities, and viewpoints are concerned. This in turn will wake us up to our own uniqueness and this continues as a cycle.

Mudita is the Buddhist concept of feeling joy for another's good fortune and happiness. Instead of wishing to be the people we are envious and jealous of, how about shifting our focus to feeling happy for them, instead?

Practice: Mudita - Joy in another's joy

Rejoicing in the good fortune of others in sympathetic joy is the antidote to jealousy and envy. Saying that rejoicing for our loved ones is easier, however doing it for others beyond our narrow circle of family and friends is difficult in the beginning.

Can we feel happy instead of jealous about someone's joy? We can begin this by the practice of Active Constructive Communication whenever somebody shares their good news. For e.g., saying something like "brilliant, tell me more about this".

In the beginning, you may require deliberate efforts and pretention to develop this attitude/feeling "fully". Like, whenever you see the happiness of other, start by saying I am Happy that you are Happy. You can further enhance the conversation till you reach a stage and feeling "May your happiness and good fortune increase."

BENEFITS OF DIGITAL DETOX

IMPROVE RELATIONSHIPS
Putting away cell phones during social gatherings improves the quality of conversations

MORE TIME
On an average, we spend 5 hours a day on cell phones.

IMPROVE SKILLSET
Digital devices can be smartly used to learn new skills or hone your existing skills.

REDUCES STRESS
Use of digital devices accentuated stress significantly as proven by many scientists

BOOSTS PRODUCTIVITY
Productivity and task performance increases significatntly by staying away from or using digital devices wisely

ATTENTION
Mr.PHONTASTIC

INCREASES ATTENTION
Human attention has fallen from 12 seconds to 8 seconds in the last 10 years according to a scientific study

HEALTHY SLEEP
Digital Detox improves sleep quality

BETTER HEALTH
With less stress and better sleep quality, your health condition improves dramatically.

20

SELFIE ESTEEM

*One of the deepest desires of mankind
has always been to be acknowledged.*

A socialite friend shared with me her boredom and emptiness. To distract herself, she was constantly partying to upload selfies and pictures on social media. She had managed to create an image and get enough "virtual" attention, which she thought helped her avoid seeing the challenges in her relationships and career. Her self-esteem was at its lowest; she sought help in managing and overcoming her challenges. I helped her orient towards grateful living, to be thankful for the challenges in her life that were urging her to grow, expand and find new creative ways of looking at issues. I advised her to do the Gratitude Wheel Exercise (Chapter 1) and identify the areas where she felt she lacked blessings in her life. It helped her raise her self-esteem rather than depend on her selfie esteem.

In a digital world - the number of followers, likes and approval by other people can make us confuse our identity with trying to get appreciation, love and virtual acceptance. Instead of self-love, people fall into the trap of Selfie-love which can be a form of narcissism or an innate need to get approval and love from others with a constant need to draw attention. It is always good to gratefully remember that our self-esteem depends on how we value ourselves. Giving that remote control to others to gain appreciation and approval is a sure shot way of lowering our self-worth.

Gratitude and self-love go hand in hand. Expressing gratitude boosts self-esteem, which in turn helps build and strengthen self-love. Often, people tend to focus on their failure or negative experiences, forgetting to learn to be grateful for the good things in life. Gratitude reverses that and puts you on a path toward self-love and a positive outlook.

The chief assailants of gratitude are envy, greed, pride, and narcissism. All these states serve as incubators for ingratitude. It is important to be aware of them and recognize them. We need not fear that they carry the power to sabotage our gratitude practice. When we focus on our blessings, learning, mercies, and protections, ingratitude has an immediate exit.

Gratitude teaches us to accept our bodies the way they are. It's important to accept and love yourself as you are today. Practicing gratitude makes you realize that you are lucky to experience good health and that your body is amazing. Accepting yourself as you are and being thankful for it is a vital step towards mental and physical well-being.

Most people's hunger for name, fame, recognition and even legacy emanates from the desire to be acknowledged.

Like me in the past, suicidal, depressed people tend to ignore their self-worth. The vicious loop of negativity can be silenced by gratitude affirmation, creating a list of good things and focusing on the working functional parts of one's life. Like the famous Zen saying goes, we cannot pour from an empty cup; we cannot be appreciative and grateful to others before we are grateful and appreciative towards ourselves.

Multiple studies on the connection between gratitude and suicide ideation have shown that being grateful leads to an increase in self-worth and self-image leading to decrease in suicide ideation. The vocabulary of negativity that the inner critic can use during self-talk can be silenced by gratitude.

Our relationship with ourselves defines our experience of life. The idea of not being good enough will let life challenges get the better of us. In bad times and struggles, a gratitude mantra that works unfailingly for me is: "this too shall pass".

Practice: Grateful Self-Acceptance

Often we are our worst critics. But self-worth can be increased by replacing a positive grateful affirmation every time your inner critic raises self-doubts and comes in the way of your efforts.

Let us have self-appreciation breaks to praise and congratulate ourselves for even the smallest achievements, to look at ourselves differently. Replacing thoughts around perfection with "This is good enough" and the affirmation of "This is perfect and joyfully improving" will help us on the path to greater self-acceptance.

A fun and effective way of reminding ourselves to experience thankfulness is to take a 'Gratitude Selfie', taking a moment to ask ourselves "Am I being grateful to myself?"

**SEEK
YOUR
SELF**

VISUALIZE
*As you awake, take a
moment to visualize the
day's positive events.*

WRITE A GRATITUDE JOURNAL
*Write down all the moments
that inspire Gratitude and lift
yourself up, right from significant happenings to
little moments.*

FOCUS ON GOALS
*Write down at least one
goal for you to accom-
plish that day*

**REFLECT ON
YOUR PROGRESS**
*As you have dinner with
family or friends, talk about
the things you most enjoyed
about your day.*

GRATEFUL
without
EXPECTATIONS

PRACTICS AFFIRMATIONS
*Practice affirmations every
morning. Choose something
simple but positive like
"Today will be a wonderful
day"*

BE KIND TO YOURSELF
*To maintain good mood and
spread positive energy, try
spending your lunch hour be
as kind as possible to
yourself.*

**DO RANDOM ACTS
OF KINDNESS**
*Challenge yourself to do as
many random acts of kindness
as you can.*

SPREAD POSITIVE ENERGY
*Greet your colleagues and other
people in your day - to - day life
with as positive energy as possible.*

*If we create everything with our thought then why not focus on posi-
tive, high quality, productive and serving thoughts. When we are
grateful without expectations, we come from a space of abundance
than from a space of lack.*

21

INNER ABUNDANCE

*Abundance is not manifested; it is
a natural state of the universe.*

My grandfather's sister was suffering from cancer in the last months of her life. She chose the Jain practice of Sallekhana, also known as Samadhi-marana of voluntarily fasting unto death. It involves embracing death by not extending life through medication, and choosing to go peacefully without lusting for the last breath of air when you know that the time is near. I knew her to be someone who had regularly practiced her morning meditation (samayak) and evening forgiveness prayer (pratikraman). Her gratitude and forgiveness practices contributed deeply to her life and impacted mine. I learnt from this that it is in our hands to choose the quality of our death and also life.

She lived a life of abundance even with very minimal resources. I learnt from her that abundance is the inner quality of peace, tranquility, contentment and being at peace with all that we have.

All of my learning for the last few years had been about how the external world reflects our inner self. The true transformation of recognizing abundance is on the inside, the outer manifestation begins the moment our inner being chooses to recognize that abundance. We recognize that it is not something to manifest and get into, it already is. We live in an abundant universe, and the lack we perceive is what we create because of hoarding and accumulation; of confusing between our needs and wants, in a state of feeling 'not enough'.

The three elemental fears that we have are the fear of death, the lack of love and the loss of identity. These cause us to exist in a state of perpetual scarcity. The idea of lack of something is wired in our evolutionary brain that helped us survive, thrive and innovate as a species. We tend to view the world through a lens of lack. However, the universe is the expression of abundance. We don't enjoy the true abundance of what life has to offer and hence keep our ideas limited to lack and tie our happiness to material things. Gratitude will help you be less materialistic. Grateful people have also been found to be more focused and productive - traits that certainly help in career advancement. People who are grateful may end up making more money. Isn't it a cool idea? (Just don't do it with expectations!)

If we tunnel our focus on the lack of things in life, we will grow more aware of all that we think we still have to strive to own. With all this we are sinking deeper into the swamp of lack. Instead if we were to focus and love what we already have then life might acquire a deeper meaning. Our existence would have a higher purpose. We need to do things we love not love the things we own. The pleasure with things we own diminishes after a while. This is the law of diminishing returns, like a child who has had a new toy for a while does not find it interesting anymore. On the other hand, if we strive to remain joyful in any situation, the external factors have minimal impact on our state of being.

When we recognize our gifts, blessings and uniqueness we are in tune with the philosophy of 'I am complete'. From this strong foundation, we can surpass our limiting beliefs, self-doubts and negativity to reach a state of inner abundance and joy. Gratitude requires compassion for the self and tolerance for others. It gives us the ability to understand the abundance of our inner gifts, our uniqueness.

The resource on the next page shares the seven spiritual laws of abundance.

Practice: Magnifying Gratitude

A different tactic of magnifying gratitude is by starting small. Decide to think and start small instead of lofty big goals.

It means acknowledging that we feel pretty thankless at the moment, and then looking around for some little thing to appreciate.

Here are some examples:

Thinking big: "I should be grateful every single day that I live in a nice house with my own backyard."

Starting small: "That's a pretty little bird in the yard."

Thinking big: "I must never forget to be thankful that my children are supportive."

Starting small: "That was nice of my daughter to text me today."

7 SPIRITUAL LAWS
OF
ABUNDANCE

1. THE LAW OF EXCHANGE
(GIVE > < RECEIVING)
*The Universe operates in
giving and receiving*

2. THE LAW OF ECHO
*Everything that manifests around you
is an echo of your inner state*

3. THE LAW OF DETACHMENT
*What you receive is proportional to
your level of detachment from the reward*

4. THE LAW OF EXPONENTIALITY
*In a conscious Universe, receiving is
exponential to giving*

5. THE LAW OF NON - LOCALITY
*Giving and receiving are
non - local in time and space.*

6. THE LAW OF DHARMA
*The Universe brings to you all the resources
You need in order to live your purpose*

7. THE LAW OF INEXHAUSTIBILITY
*What is inexhaustible when shared is wealth,
what is exhaustible when shared is a resource*

**From my teacher and brother Sujith Ravindran's book, The Seven
Spiritual Laws of Abundance.*

PART 4 : <u>**A**PPRECIATION</u>
EXPRESSING

Mr. Expressive

ZERO COMPLAINT LIFE

Chapters

ZERO
COMPLAINT LIFE

Practices

Complaint Free Gratitude Band
Radical Honesty
Gratitude Gifts
Vocabulary of Thankfulness
Public Display of Appreciation
Social Gratitude
Habit Stacking

Mr. Expressive

22

4 CS - COMPLAINING, CRIBBING, CURSING, CRITICIZING

Criticizing without malice is the finest form of appreciation.

One of my friends used to call me his 3 AM friend. Truth be told, he would call just to complain and crib about all that was wrong in his life. All his interactions had the same theme, him being a victim. Listening to him and holding a space of empathy wasn't helping his complaining habit. I came across a book, A Complaint Free World by Pastor Will Bowen, in which he talks about using a bracelet to become aware of when we are complaining. This idea inspired me so profoundly that I experimented with myself and many others and saw positive results. Pastor Will Bowen also founded the Complaint Free Movement.

Why do we complain? We complain when we experience dissatisfaction, grief or are hurt. Studies show that bottling up one's emotions can shorten lifespan by an average of two years. Complaining has a purpose of keeping the heart clean. A better way is to keep the source itself clean, filled with gratitude. We all need the ritual of letting off steam to maintain a healthy balance of thoughts, desires, needs, wants, actions and disappointments and frustrations. But in today's world that has become an epidemic of sorts threatening our very existence. Everywhere you see - especially TV news, which thrives on the amplification of fear - there seem to be negativity.

Complaining is good only when it leads to inspired action and is given without malice to someone with an intention of bringing about betterment. Our words impact our reality. Complaining creates a world of discontentment, negativity and unhappiness around us, turning it into a habitual response, far removed from our true nature of joy and peace. New neural pathways are created in our brain every time we commit an act. Therefore, by indulging in cribbing, complaining and criticizing habitually, we are not only creating new yet faulty neural networks but also reinforcing them.

So how does one get rid of this negative habit? The answer is to detox. We can unlearn this habit and replace it with a simple act of being grateful. Gratitude is the antidote for complaining, the source of which is unfulfilled expectations, needs and wants.

We all have someone on whose shoulder we feel comfortable enough to cry while complaining - common dislikes are a great connection point for people to unite with each other just like liking something can connect us. What we are primarily trying to achieve through the process of complaining is gaining sympathy, attention, an acknowledgement of our victimhood and indulgence in self-pity. Unless we detox, we cannot get to the stage of feeling good about ourselves.

It is the vibration of gratitude that offers a solution to the harmful effects of complaining on the brain. A moment-to-moment living in gratitude acts as an emotional trampoline which provides the balance and buffer to deal with harmful effects of complaining. The 80-20 rule applies to complaining as well. We complain about most things in our lives and appreciate very little of what we have.

Follow the sandwich model while criticizing. The soft patty is the criticism and the outer layers are appreciation, like a sandwich wrap. Those who are successful in dealing with people will tell you that when criticism is wrapped in appreciation, there is a much higher chance of acceptance of the feedback prompting change from negativity to positivity in thoughts and action.

Practice: Complaint Free Gratitude Band

Words have the power to influence our thoughts and actions. The more we complain and brood over things the more we give power to negativity.

Wear a Complaint Free Gratitude band - it can be a watch, a bangle, a bracelet or an elastic band that can be worn around the wrist and switched to the other each time you complain.

The first time I tried a Complaint Free Gratitude Band, I had to switch the band 32 times in a day, every time I realized I was using words and thoughts that amounted to complaining. Can you keep the band around one wrist for a whole week? (i.e. without complaining even once).

Get your own orange silicon band stamped with words Complaint - free Gratitude at http://www.vitamingratitude.com

COMPLAINT-FREE GRATITUDE BAND

A tool for becoming aware of our complaining words.
When we change our words, our thoughts and our reality changes.

| CONCEPT | = | 7 DAYS IN SINGLE HAND WITHOUT A CHANGE |
| CHANGE OF HAND | → | EVERY TIME YOU COMPLAIN |

Use a simple bracelet/bangle/watch/rubber band. Take on a challenge to go without complaining for at least a week. Each time you complain, switch the band to the other wrist and start again. Increase the No Complaint Challenge period to a month and gradually longer periods. You will reach the stage of a Zero Complaint Life.

Definition of Complaint

Describing an event or a person negatively without telling what is required to fix the problem. The constructive complaint has to be oriented towards the person who can solve it.

23

SWIMMING IN SHALLOW GRATITUDE

Every marathon runner first started by faltering with baby steps.

At the beginning of their gratitude practice, a lot of people practice what I call 'pretend' or 'show off gratitude'. Some people consider this shallow and fake. Many look down on it. However, I am a big believer of the fake-it-till-you-make-it-real mantra. Starting with pretending to be grateful can eventually lead you to the path of actual gratefulness.

Gratitude practiced even for show off can never be untrue. By practicing and starting in this manner, we pave the way for gratitude to come into our being. Fake it till you make it and pretend till it becomes an unconscious habit is a dictum that I believe in. For starters, this is a great method of expression and I whole heartedly encourage it. Pretending to be grateful works in the short term but eventually we recognize its true benefits. The journey from 'pretending to being' takes time, patience, nurturing, and loving encouragement like we would give to a child taking their first few faltering steps before they walk and run with full speed.

Benedictine monk David Steindl-Rast states, "Our initial forays are a pretence, they are not a native behavior of authenticity, but they are good to take one's first steps towards a life entrenched with gratitude. Acting-as-if is also a great way to do so."

Our survival brains are tuned to being risk averse and protection is a survival based mechanism born out of fear. Negativity and fear in our amygdala (part of the brain which has a primary role in the processing of memory, decision-making, and emotional reactions) are a reality of our animal nature. In our gratitude mindset, things work in much the same way when we force ourselves to smile or listen to happy music when we're feeling sad: it stimulates the part of the brain associated with positive emotions .If you're grateful, you're not fearful, and if you're not fearful, you're not violent. If you're grateful, you act out of a sense of adequacy, not scarcity and are willing to share.

Our physiology can change our moods. Our words, thoughts, actions and feelings are interlinked. Gradually, from saying we move to doing. For when we say and repeat it for a long time, we absorb it. Gradually our behavior (a reflection of our nature and habits) and actions also change. There is a transformation of our feelings and thoughts; there is a shift in our mindset and heart. Humans have this ability to engineer the mind for specific outcomes. Reiterating and reinforcing out-comes leads to action. So instead of pressuring yourself, you can start practicing gratitude from whatever point you wish, at whatever pace and intensity you want.

Competence comes with practice. We move from a zone of unconscious ignorance where we are not even aware of the fact that we don't know, to unconscious competence, where we are so skilled that we are on an auto pilot mode - where our words, actions, feelings and thoughts are aligned towards living with gratitude.

Don't be perturbed about how much to practice and the level of shallowness which may exist in your expression of gratitude. Over time, when practiced with awareness, being thankful will become second nature and your practice will automatically acquire depth. You can learn to practice from splashing in the shallow pools to diving in the deep oceans of grateful living. I recommend the practice of radical honesty. For some people the whole idea of 'pretending as if' doesn't feel good and I have tried the opposite of this as a gratitude practice, which is the practice of radical honesty.

Practice: Radical Honesty

When there is a misalignment between what we wish to project about ourselves and what the reality is, we end up being dishonest. Lying is one of the main causes of human distress and it is a destroyer of relationships and reputations. It can also lead to a feeling of alienation and loneliness as you avoid people and their curiosity about you and your life.

Practice being honest and authentic in what you say and do. Initially, it might be difficult and challenging. It will cause a lot of anxiety and perhaps a sense of inadequacy. Gradually, it is possible to appreciate how free, light it can make you feel.

This practice is for those who lie to avoid confrontations or cannot assert themselves or are obsessed about keeping up with appearances.

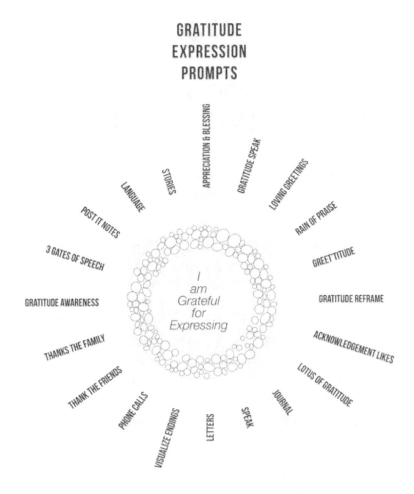

GRATITUDE
EXPRESSION
PROMPTS

We are looking for meaning and purpose for our lives and our life is the major expression of our existence. Can we reflect upon how we use our words, communication and actions to the world?

24

THE OCEAN OF
UNEXPRESSED GRATITUDE

When I was born my first breath couldn't have said thank you,
before I die let my every breath be one of thankfulness

One of my friends, a participant in my workshop was having a turbulent relationship with his father. After three long years of working with him on this issue, their relationship finally acquired some semblance of normalcy. Yet, he couldn't somehow articulate his feelings and show love to his father. I had him do an exercise of writing a gratitude letter, focusing on their precious time together when he was a child. Although his childhood was filled with separation, loneliness and abandonment, he did have many things to thank his parents for. My friend managed to write the letter but just didn't have the courage to send it. Sadly, his father passed away while the letter was still with him. He never got a chance to express his love and gratitude to his father.

William Arthur, oft quoted writer of inspirational writings, said, "Feeling gratitude and not expressing it is like wrapping a present and not giving it". When we do not express our feelings, they stay hidden in the safety locker of our hearts, only to cause regret later.

Whatever the reason or excuse we give ourselves, gratitude which remains unexpressed only causes damage. We swim in an ocean of unexpressed gratitude, afraid of giving and receiving gratitude for the fear of being vulnerable. A friend of mine would never mention good things or happy events for the fear that it might attract bad luck. Many still knock on wood while sharing blessings, fearing they will attract something evil. Unexpressed emotions and feelings often also lead to misinterpretation. As a result, we might come across as ungrateful or lose a valuable relationship altogether. Expressing gratitude brings joy and elevates our energy to a higher level.

A lot of us are afraid to express gratitude, especially at the workplace. Very often, managers and leaders are reluctant to show appreciation fearing requests for pay hikes during appraisal time or over confident employees underperforming. Sometimes, we feel that showing appreciation and gratitude will make people take advantage of us.

There is no appropriate moment or time to express gratitude. The intensity of the feeling diminishes as time passes while you wait for the right moment to find the right words. Another participant in my workshop was reluctant to write his gratitude letter because his handwriting was illegible. He managed to type it after much persuasion. Fear of rejection is another barrier which stops people from expressing themselves. All one needs is to open their heart - with a shot of courage, if needed - before reaching out to another person.

Here is why we also resist gratitude that comes our way:

- Fear of rejection
- Childhood conditioning
- Being too attached to one person (usually a parent, sibling, or a teacher) which makes it difficult to imagine

life with another.

- Apprehension about over compensation and inadequacy i.e. Will I be able to reciprocate the same?

If you have felt any of these at some point, you may find it difficult to accept appreciation. For many, receiving gratitude is not as easy as expressing it. Many people are surprised or embarrassed when someone gives them a compliment or gift. They may even start doubting the person's intentions, that the giver is perhaps expecting a favor in return.

Practice: Gratitude Gifts

Regardless of the occasion, gifts are always welcome. Giving gifts to acknowledge loved ones and colleagues for their support, a successful idea, unconditional cooperation, diligence or timely help etc. can go a long way in relationship building.

It is genuine recognition and expression of a person's significance in one's life. What matters is not the value of the gift but the sentiment behind it.

It is easy to give gratitude gifts if we can focus on the other person's preferences, likes and dislikes. Some people prefer useful gifts instead of a perishable gift like flowers; some prefer keepsakes, mementoes and remembrance gifts rather than something that is ornate, fancy and expensive. Some prefer handmade gifts and cards etc. In an increasing virtual world, give gifts of gratitude.

SEA OF UNEXPRESSED APPRECIATION

Not expressing our gratitude and appreciation leads to regret later. Hiding our emotions of gratefulness in the safety locker of our heart is like buying a gift and not giving it.

25

LANGUAGES OF GRATITUDE

*Kindness, compassion and grace are
the universal languages of gratitude.*

A visit to Oman for setting up our international cloud computing business in the Middle East enriched me with a lesson of a lifetime. Roaming the streets, my cabbie and I couldn't find the way to where I had to go since the GPS is not very helpful in the labyrinth of by-lanes there. In a street full of houses, we ended up asking many people for directions since we were thoroughly lost. Whenever we stopped to ask for directions, the guard at a house would exchange pleasantries with us, ask after our health and only then guide us with directions, post which, it was a round of heartfelt thankyous and byes. I was amused at first but was getting more anxious later since each of these 'ceremonial' stops was eating away precious minutes and I had to reach where I had to on time. In hindsight, I realize that using a grateful demeanor and language towards an unexpected guest was the culture here and a way of grateful living.

Language has a strong impact on our thoughts, which in turn create our reality. Maya Angelou, American poet, suggests that our deepest yearning is:

- Do you see me?
- Do you care that I am here?
- Am I enough for you or do you need me to be better in some way?
- Can I tell that I'm special to you by the way you look at me?

The answers to these questions connect us to everyone around us, and decide the quality of our relationship with ourselves and others.

When we use words of blessings and thankfulness like I'm so fortunate, I always attract abundance, I hold gratitude for my challenges, we create a reality in our mind and in the external world that is filled with joy. When we are critical of ourselves and others, our language resembles, I am always late, I have butter fingers, I am accident-prone; we end up reinforcing a belief system that is self-sabotaging. When I changed my self-talk with the language of gratitude, I noticed a shift in my feelings, my world view and my external world.

Gratitude vocabulary is the five ways in which we show love and appreciation. Author Gary Chapman espouses the five languages of love framework - words, touch, acts of service, time, and gifts. I've added a sixth - attention.

Attention is one of the most effective tools in your arsenal of relationship building. The gratitude language of attention leads to deep listening that is beyond the spoken words. In a world of increasing information overload, offering your undivided attention is truly valuable and precious.

A few words of praise can make a mother feel appreciated for the meal she has cooked. Genuine praise can only come if you are paying attention to the effort and love that goes into something. Words of support, encouragement and appreciation are expressions of gratitude. They make an individual feel valued. Equally important is the tone in which we speak, the body language and eye contact.

A reassuring hand placed on the shoulder, a hug, a kiss, a handshake, making love; these are all ways of sharing emotions - a simple way to express gratitude. Something that I practice regularly is the gratitude hug, the kind that lasts beyond half a minute.

A helping hand is another way of showing appreciation and thankfulness to someone, besides giving gifts. Gratitude when accompanied by a gift becomes a memory of appreciation.

Practice: Vocabulary of Thankfulness

Gratitude begins in our heart and finds expression in words.

In your interactions, use words of appreciation, praise, curiosity, happiness, joy. This creates an environment that fosters happiness and confidence. If our conversation is interspersed with positive words, e.g. how wonderful, we will find ourselves much more open and connected.

Make a list of thankful words, appreciative words and sentences and phrases of good fortune/luck and affirmations. Avoid negative statements about yourself and the habits you don't like.

Grateful people use a vocabulary of blessings to express themselves. It can improve our own well-being as well as that of people we are grateful towards.

WORDS
OF
THANKFULNESS

*Write here the words of Thankfulness that you would like
to add to vocabulary.*

*Words of Thankfulness include using a vocabulary of wonderment,
curiosity, happiness and joy; wonderful, excellent, great job, I am
proud of you, nice, blessed, fortunate etc. are words that can not
only change our outlook of focussing on gratitude but always rewire
our brain towards positivity, openness and acceptance.*

26

THE ART & SCIENCE OF APPRECIATION

*Specific and timely appreciation
from the heart gratifies the soul.*

At one of my gratitude events for a corporate organization, the purchase manager of this large MNC shared his story of having worked for 20 years with the same organization. He said that he had received a handwritten gratitude letter from the owner of the company, detailing his initial years and the sacrifices he had made for the company. It brought tears to his eyes at these sincere words of praise. Even though he had received many awards and a fantastic salary, a home and an office with a view, his boss had never really shared praise for his efforts.

Sometimes we don't articulate what we feel, assuming that our loved ones already know how we feel. Our love for them is a fact because of our actions. Words of appreciation to our parents, friends and colleagues can help us better acknowledge the gratitude we feel; unexpressed gratitude is like a wrapped gift never given.

Appreciation is the highest quality of gratitude. When we express gratitude -verbally or otherwise - we cater to one of the highest needs of a human being, that of being recognized and valued. Voltaire once said "Appreciation is a wonderful thing. It makes what is excellent in others belong to us as well". What we appreciate in others reflects in us. When appreciating others, we are essentially recognizing that value within us too. It is a recognition and acknowledgment of someone's highest self by us. Feedback is another important tool of appreciation. Online feedback can make or break a brand, whether it is a person or an organization.

It is also imperative that we balance appreciation with constructive criticism, both for ourselves and others. Criticism without malice is the sincerest form of appreciation; it encourages and inspires the best in a person.

Remember to follow the principle of SAGAT while appreciating. Specific for the person to know what exactly you liked; Authentic, which is real instead of fake and insincere; Genuine or unconditional; Appropriate as in neither over the top nor too generic; Timely, as too late or too early, and the other person may not feel its value.

When we hear a great singer, watch a play or are moved by a movie, our appreciation is limited to claps, a standing ovation, raving about it on social media or giving word of mouth publicity. But are all these enough to the overfilling joy that you feel at the end of performance, can it be repaid in any way? Words and our gestures of appreciation sometimes don't do justice to the quality of what we receive at such moments. Sometimes when we don't express and the moment passes away, all that is left is a bitter taste of regret. In the sea of unexpressed appreciation lies the debris of regret.

Some people are very miserly with their words of praise,

hoarding and using them very sparingly, so as not to over-indulge the other person. I've seen disciplined parents being so selective with their words of support, encouragement and appreciation that the child eventually feels unloved and not worthy enough.

Some of us have trouble receiving appreciation and either bury ourselves in the ground with humility and humbleness or go to the other extreme of "tell me more". Some people are so realistic that they neither have the fear of criticism nor are they swayed by the hypnotism of praise.

We can easily appreciate what we like. Can we also appreciate the mundane, the regular, the imperfect, the things that we dislike?

Practice: Public Display of Appreciation

Immerse a person in a shower of appreciation.

Stand in a circle surrounding a person whose birthday or anniversary it is. Each member of the family or group needs to say words of appreciation and praise for the person.

These words and blessings need to be authentic and expressed in a unique way by each person. Those who are not used to praising others need to put in extra effort to be expressive. Such a shower of appreciation can be more valuable than any material gift.

This practice, along with creating goodwill and camaraderie, forges a culture of appreciation and encouraging the good in others. For large groups, write something about the person, and then read a few random wishes.

ART
OF
APPRECIATION

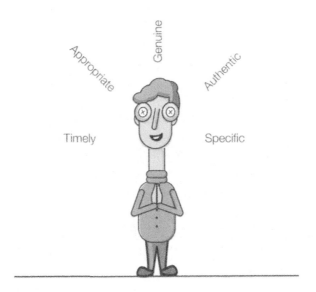

 **APPRECIATION**
Mr. EXPRESSIVE

Gratitude teaches us to appreciate what we have before time makes us appreciate what we had. When we appreciate a circumstance, person or an event we have to authentic so that it doesn't come across as fake. Appreciation should be genuine so that the other person doesn't feel it is for reciprocation.

129

27

HASHTAG GRATITUDE

The pro-social nature of gratitude gets amplified and resonates in a virtual and more connected world.

A year ago, I launched the hash tag #artofappreciation - an invitation to people on Facebook to tag them and I promised to comment on them. The challenge was to talk about their inner qualities, values and behavior rather than comment about their clothes, smile or appearance. It took me 48 hours to do this for 150 people who had tagged themselves. It taught me that people love to be appreciated and in the digital world where there is a readymade audience, showing appreciation is even easier. While the hash tag went viral and many people took up this challenge, my intention was that it should lead to specific, authentic and genuine praise.

Facebook has turned us into "like" addicts, with the thumbs up symbol becoming a general acknowledgement of others, sometimes even a non-verbal conversation closer. Even gratitude in the digital medium is often times only a show of accomplishments. Relationships, success, achievements for some of us are starting to become true only when shared on social media. On a positive side, it has also made it possible for us to show our gratefulness and appreciation by tagging those who have supported us as a medium of expression of our gratefulness - it's faster, has a wider outreach and more convenient.

The first thing we check in the morning after waking up is the number of notifications on the phone. So when I turned to grateful living, I created my phone wallpapers using quotes on gratitude and the reminder notifications were for my gratitude practices.

The digital world is also a place to expand our circle of gratitude. A few months back, I started a Facebook group called "The Circle of Gratitude" - a community for sharing gratitude practices with hundreds of gratitude exercises and over a thousand people participating. A few group members also took up the 365-day Challenge of Random Acts of Kindness; caring for and healing animals as a way of expressing gratitude. The gratitude exercises suggested in the book have been honed by the feedback I received from this group. Every day, hundreds share their expression of gratitude through this circle.

Sharing, liking, following, and commenting on posts has a positive association - for those who post and for those who respond. Research shows that the level of a user's self-disclosure on social media is associated with the user's level of personal meaning in life. Social media becomes an open and easier space for even the shy to express and appreciate.

In a digital world today, people wake up to looking at their phone and notifications before they look at anything else. We talk in emoticons rather than in true emotions. I started a company called gifting happiness because I felt that the virtual world was increasingly moving away from visiting friends and family, gifting and interacting in non-virtual ways. From well-wishers who would visit to greet and share, we have turned into wall wishers on birthdays. From calling on the phone, we have turned app yappers on festivals and holidays. On social media before posting something that you are grateful for, a simple check would help. Consider whether the post will invoke inspiration or envy. Otherwise, it will end up falling in the category of show-off gratitude. Gratitude is a natural filter of positivity framing our world view. It is not denial; it is the fact that we can recognize good in the worst of situations. Gratitude is contagious; it can inspire you and others around you as well as amplify the joy in your heart.

Practice: Social Gratitude

Join or start a group for cultivating and practicing gratitude. On the internet, you can find numerous hash tags, quotes, activities and interactive groups besides a wealth of knowledge for practicing gratitude.

Facebook groups like the community I run (http://www.fb.com/groups/circleofgratitude) can help create a group of likeminded people, inspiring a community that practices gratitude. Digital apps like the Gratsapp can be used for gratitude journaling. Lots of Instagrammers take the 365-Days gratitude challenge - taking pictures of things that they are grateful for, or of their random acts of kindness to put up and share.

These groups act as a support network and ensure that when you feel like giving up, you are always motivated to keep at it.

50 DAYS
OF DAILY GRATITUDE
CHALLENGES

1. Why start this challenge?

2. Spouse or significant other

3. Family

4. A family member

5. Something someone gave you

6. The city you love in

7. A friend

8. Express Gratitude to 3 people

9. How did you do and feel?

10. List 5 things you like about you

11. Someone who inspires you

12. Your favorite personality trait

13. A challenge you have overcome

14. A talent you have

15. Things you like about spring

16. Simple things in life

17. Something you take for granted

18. The weather

19. Health

20. Another friend

21. Things you like about Summer

22. Something you use every day

23. Favorite physical trait

24. A book you learned from

25. Education

26. Favorite spot in your city

27. Your past

28. Your favorite memory

29. Your current age

30. Core value

31. A city you have visited

32. Something you look forward to

33. Things you like about fall

34. Your neighborhood

35. Your home

36. Something you created

37. Music you love

38. Your heritage

39. Greatest accomplishment

40. Hobbies

41. Your Favorite possession

42. A mentor/teacher

43. Your favorite holiday

44. What you do for fun

45. Technology

46. Someone you got to meet

47. Your job

48. Lessons learned this year

49. 100 things to be thankful for

50. Did this challenge change you?

*Prompts to be Thankful for each single day for a 50 day challenge.
You can put the answers in your journal, social media or reflect on them.*

28

SERIAL HABITUAL GRATITUDER

To train the evolutionary survival oriented brain towards gratitude takes sustained effort, focus and practice.

As a keynote speaker at a cloud technology event, I was once introduced as a serial habitual entrepreneur and I joked back that I was a parallel entrepreneur as I was running five companies in different domains. I took to entrepreneurship rather early in life, right from my teenage days but my story of becoming a serial habitual Gratituder was one dotted with failures and false starts, just like my endeavor to setup a morning 60-min power hour of me time - 20 minutes of meditation, 20 minutes of physical activity and 20 minutes of inspirational reading and videos. It was easier said than done. My work, travels, health and life circumstances would invariably force me to postpone or wait for an appropriate divine alignment of constellations before I could begin. And when I did I found the time too long, wasn't able to keep myself motivated or consistent at all. I would find a variety of excuses and justify to myself and friends on why I wasn't following my own advice. I realized that I needed to start small and stack habits for a behavioral shift.

Practicing gratitude consciously is a new change. The brain will take time to acclimatize and adapt to it. Even if you fail 99 times out of a 100, focus on that one time when you succeeded feeling grateful. If nothing else, at least give credit for the effort that you have put in. Begin with the small things in your control. If you miss one day of gratitude practice, say "cancel" three times in your head and wipe the slate clean. Start afresh. Be grateful to yourself for failing and reattempting. Stack your new endeavor with a habit you already have - it could be anything from brushing your teeth or any other daily ritual. I set about habit stacking, adding a habit on top of one I already had to start on my path of gratitude.

According to behavioral scientist Dr. BJ Fogg, any habit is fuelled by 3 elements: motivation, ability, and trigger. If you keep the activity so small that it sounds laughable to practice, you will be motivated to start it. For instance, to make counting your blessings a daily habit, start by counting just one thing you are grateful for after you have eaten breakfast or started your car. Take your tiny habit and stack it atop a regular habit. Your current habit forms the trigger for the new tiny habit.

Teaching also helped me make grateful living a habit and find discipline. By teaching others to learn it and with small incremental steps of trying a variety of practices of my own, I have zeroed in on things that suited me best and incorporated them into my life. A good physical workout causes Delayed Onset Muscle Soreness (DOMS) - your muscles start paining the day after you start your first workout. It is a sign of wear and tear of the muscle, which is essential for its growth. Similarly, with gratitude, some wear and tear and occasional sweet pain is normal.

Focus on what's going right and completely ignore the wrong for the time being. Imagine you are asked to cook a recipe you've never known before; you would be happy just to finish it. The taste of that first dish rarely matters - the cook is happy that the preparation wasn't burnt. Similarly, life won't be a paradise of positivity with just one day of practicing gratitude. Allow yourself time to get used to being thankful.

To become Serial habitual Gratituder, start with small habits, attempting multiple practices till you find the ones that resonate with you. Practice them for at least 21 days and deepen them with higher span, intensity and complexity. Slowly you'll move to a zone of unconscious competence and they will end up not just a part of doing, but also of your being. What first step are you going to take today on this path?

Practice: Habit Stacking

Forming new habits can be painful with the possibility of disappointment. The Tiny habits method consists of Reminder, Routine, and Reward. When I started writing this book, I would tell myself every day: "after waking up every day, I will write one paragraph at least." Keep the goal tiny till the mind adapts to it, motivated by triggering it to an already existing habit and finally giving yourself a reward.

How about: "after opening my eyes and before looking towards notifications on phone, I will think of at least one blessing that I am grateful for". This is a tiny habit that I have encouraged many teenagers to practice that has helped them to become more positive and grateful.

HABIT
OF
GRATITUDE

REMINDER
The cue or trigger that starts the habit.
Example: Traffic light turns green.

ROUTINE

REWARD

The action you take.
The habit itself
Example: You drive
through intersection.

The benefit you gain from
doing the habit.
Example: You get closer to
destination.

THE 3 R'S
OF HABIT
FORMATION

3R Framework from B. J. Foggs, Tiny Habits

PART 5 : **A**CTION
DOING

Major. Strong

MAXMISE THE
QUALITY OF YOUR LIFE

Chapters

Facing Life's Major Challenges

Taken for Granted in Relationships

Super Wellbeing

The Grateful Workplace

Vitamin M for Money

Pay it Forward Parenting

Redefining Success

MAXMISE THE
QUALITY OF YOUR LIFE

Practices

Rear View Mirror of Gratitude

Mental Subtraction

Gratitude Water, Sleep and Food Grace

Culture of Gratitude and Gratitude Week

Reverse Bucket List

Jar of Awesomeness and Gratitude Games

Success Visualisation

Major. Strong

29

FACING LIFE'S MAJOR CHALLENGES

In the rear-view mirror of life it is easy to be grateful, what takes courage is being grateful in the moment.

Kiran Kanojia is India's first woman blade runner. She lost a leg in a train accident. In an interview, I asked her if she was grateful for her challenges. Here's what she said: "I am grateful to be able to live my life, having loving parents, meeting and connecting with people, learning how they overcame their challenges. Once we accept the problems we have in life, we can overcome them and achieve our ambitions. The small things in life give immense happiness which we often tend to miss. Had I given up after the accident, I would not have been running and be known as a blade runner. Life isn't easy, but it's not very tough either. It's we who complicate it."

Compare a current skill of yours which you are good at with the level you were at when you were learning it. A cook doesn't become a master chef without more than a few burnt dishes; a toddler doesn't learn walking overnight. Many people are hard on themselves when they fail. Give yourself time to overcome challenges. Being grateful is all about focusing on challenges that you have overcome. There can be no next class or level without an exam. The point is to find your lotus in the mud, your oasis in the desert.

Our greatest challenge is also our greatest blessing. These challenges help us grow, deepen our wisdom, expand horizons and alter our perspectives. I consider my daughter and my relationship with her as my greatest challenge and also my greatest blessing. Understanding her has expanded the meaning of love and commitment for me. I must say that I've grown a notch in life from it.

When you look in the rear-view mirror of your life, you realize that your challenges have helped your growth. Without challenges in life, one stops growing. We stop improving and become stagnant. Challenges fuel our growth to greatness. A challenge can be an opportunity for us to discover inherent strengths. Challenges deserve gratitude; they propel us to reach the next level as a human spirit.

How do you handle challenges? Challenges of health teach us to be more careful with our food choices, to nurture and pamper our bodies, to respect the body as a temple to the soul. Challenges in relationships are a mirror for us to clear our biases, work on our weaknesses and let go of the past. Challenges with career and money teach us to learn new skills, upgrade knowledge and turn into more efficient professionals. When we are grateful to these lessons that come our way, our spirit grows and the boundaries of heart, mind and body expand. When you view from the perspective of gratitude, all challenges are opportunities.

Gratefulness shouldn't be saved just for the 'big deals'. An ideal approach to receiving the rewards of appreciation is to look for new things to be thankful for. Whenever we look at the rear-view mirror of our life we realize that we wouldn't be in our current state of achievement or level of happiness if it were not for the lessons of past challenges. Being grateful to our challenges gives us the ability to be equanimous towards both good and bad, success and failure.

Our karma and actions define our dharma and life purpose, when we go from being furious about our challenges to being curious about them. Gratitude gives us the perspective to ask our life's major challenges 'what they teach' instead of saying 'why me' or', what have I done to deserve this misfortune'.

Practice: Rear View Mirror of Gratitude

Challenges and opportunities are two sides of the same coin.

When you are facing a challenge, or have just come out of it, take out time for gratitude reflection. Sit in a relaxed position and take a deep breath. Become aware of things around your immediate environment like the air we breathe, things we smell/ hear/ feel. Then, say thankful words for them to yourself. Write down the list of challenges you are facing on one side and the probable list of opportunities that can help you get out from such challenging situations. Feel the gratitude for these opportunities; they will help you equalize the negatives with positives.

Remembering gratefully how we have learned and grown from our previous challenges will help us find courage and strength for the present one.

142

PROMPTS
FOR
CHALLENGES

Express your gratitude towards these challenges

30

TAKEN FOR GRANTED
IN RELATIONSHIPS

*How can we really take for granted anything when
the ultimate truth is even our next breathe is a gift.*

Some of the most insightful learning can come from a source least expected. In hind sight, I think of my 90-year-old grandmother's life as a lesson, but it was her death that taught me something deeply valuable. I was inconsolable on the day she died, but also realized just how impermanent our very existence is. It's easy to take life for granted, especially when you are young and reckless. It's also easy to take for granted our natural resources, life sustenance and the earth itself. Ever thought of how perfect the distance of the earth is from the sun or the beautiful balance of ecology on the planet to support billions of lives? When I decided to make the choice of a grateful living, I started to wake up to these ideas and many others like these. Every day would turn out to be a day to find something new to be thankful for.

For years, I was into mindless eating; eating while reading a book, or while fidgeting with something. I was doing everything else but eating. To me food was merely a necessary daily chore. Before long though, I had developed a thyroid disorder, vitamin deficiency and a gluten allergy. What I took for granted led me to a host of problems. After I started the gratitude practices, I started to eat mindfully, which has done wonders for my health. Gratitude is the opposite of taking something for granted, and appreciating everything from the most profound to the most mundane.

While we take others for granted and neglect them, we grow resentful when we ourselves are neglected. Being neglected, unappreciated and unvalued can lead to cracks in any relationship.

Interestingly, lottery winners mostly report being only as happy as they were before winning the lottery. Even in several abusive relationships, people resign themselves to the abuse rather than do something about it. Getting used to a life situation - good or bad - is how humans adapt. This getting used to or hedonic adaptation is a natural process of survival after being repeatedly exposed to the same emotion-producing stimulus - it happens because we tend to "experience" less of the emotion. A disabled person can have the remarkable ability to rebound and eventually be as happy as they were before their loss.

On the flipside though, it also gets us used to our amazing spouses or great jobs with the tendency of taking them for granted. To become more aware of this every day is the key to greater happiness. Gratitude is one of the most powerful tools for this. Very often, people realize the real value of what they have only after they lose it. Loss of any kind is in fact a life lesson that teaches us to be more respectful, mindful and value what we have.

Relationships are living breathing entities that must be nourished if they are to remain healthy-no matter how new or old. Gratitude is a potent nutrient; a relationship cannot grow without it. All relationships are about connection at the end of the day. Gratitude can be an important first step to establish rapport thereby creating balance. In an argument, for instance, the easiest way to do that is to pause and reflect on whether winning the argument is more important than keeping the relationship. Being grateful to the connection is the simplest way to bring back love.

Relationships end up becoming dysfunctional when one or both of the partners end up using guilt, shame, and punishment instead of thankfulness, gratitude and appreciation.

Practice: Mental Subtraction

Contemplating life without a loved one, or a limb can give us new found appreciation for something that we take for granted. While this may seem extreme, it is a great way of going beyond the mind's way of hedonic adaptation. This is like a back-door intervention for boosting gratitude. People who do this exercise tend to feel an enhanced sense of appreciation.

One argument could be that we become more mindful of the good that is already present when we contemplate its absence. This same strategy can be applied to our good fortune, people, circumstances or events to feel greater appreciation and connection, by subtracting this event and contemplating how life would be without it.

MENTAL
SUBSTRACTION
VISUALIZATION '

Reflect on a positive event in your life. For example, an educational or career achieve-ment, the birth of a child, a special trip you took. Think about all the circumstances that made this possible. Then write down all of the possible events and decisions that could have gone differently and prevented this event from occurring. Imagine what your life would be like right now if you hadn't enjoyed this positive event. You can also do this for important people in your life by reflecting on what your life would be like if you had never met this person.

31

SUPER WELL-BEING

*Gratitude improves the pace of self-healing
by focusing on positives, immunizes the body
effectively and leads to better sleep.*

One of my greatest inspirations is Nick Vujicic who was born with tetra-Amelia syndrome, a rare disorder characterized by the absence of arms and legs. His first book, Life without Limits: Inspiration for a Ridiculously Good Life is a story of hope and triumph and how to be thankful and achieve greatness despite adversity. My thankfulness for my body was reinforced on several occasions when my body would demand rest after a spell of pain and disease, by reminding me to honor it. For a long time, I was recognized by my constant coughing. In retrospect, I am thankful to the cough that was triggered by my allergies, for bringing my awareness to mindful eating and quality sleep.

A lot of people report much better quality of sleep once they are on the path to gratitude. This is a scientifically well researched fact and even intuitively we know that the contentment resulting from grateful living can help us sleep better, which in turn critically influences our health and physical well-being. Being grateful also reduces stress and steers you towards more positive thoughts. A mind that is unburdened by negative thoughts and worries tends to rest better. Gratitude helps us get superwell supersoon not because it is a placebo but rather because it triggers our body for positive outcome in the body.

When we have a lower threshold of pain we complain incessantly. But when we start living a grateful life, our complaining comes down with the immediate effect being on increasing our pain threshold. Gratitude has been found to be effective in lowering blood pressure, improving immunity, fostering healthier heart rhythms besides being linked to faster recovery from illnesses. It makes us more resilient and less susceptible to diseases.

In a 2003 report in the Journal of Personality and Social Psychology, it was found that patients having neuromuscular diseases reported a greater sense of well-being and faster recovery when they maintained gratitude journals. What's more, gratitude has been found to be effective in keeping diabetes under check as well. Subjects suffering from chronic pain and inflammation of joints reported lower body aches after they started practicing gratitude. The body is intrinsically built to heal itself and besides medication, an attitude of gratitude quickens the natural processes of the body to recover and heal. We get super well super soon with gratitude.

Besides these benefits among several others, gratitude also helps in de-addiction, something that I can personally vouch for. In fact, in the USA, Alcoholics Anonymous incorporates gratitude practice as a very important tool on the path to recovery. Oxytocin and dopamine are two hormones that are released when we perform an act of gratitude. These prevent a person from developing tolerance to alcohol's sedation; which is why people who practice gratitude can eventually give up the addiction more effectively.

For years, I used to have a rather haphazard lifestyle that involved frequent travelling and sporadic bouts of fitness regimes. Even with my gratitude practice, I found journaling quite a task. The practice that eventually became a ritual that I have not missed in the last five years is the one I do in my semi wakeful state called Gratitude Morning ritual as discussed earlier. This practice eventually helped me get fitter and achieve my optimum weight, while drastically reducing my health issues.

Practice: Gratitude Water, Sleep and Food Grace

Tag your water bottle with a 'thank you' sticker, a reminder to be grateful to have accessible drinking water. When sipping water in the morning, express gratitude for it, and the source from where it comes and how it nourishes each cell in our bodies. While taking a refreshing bath, express gratitude towards the source of water, glaciers, rivers, lakes, sea, clouds, rain etc.

Say Thank you / Grace before eating, express gratitude to the food chain and the people who toil hard to grow and prepare our food. Take the time to see and appreciate your food, inhale the aroma and savor the flavors. Have gratitude dinner with family or friends.

Counting your blessings for the day or your entire life can greatly improve the quality of sleep.

HEALTH BENEFITS OF GRATITUDE

CALMS DOWN

Cultivating Gratitude and other positive emotions can reduce stress hormones like Cortisol by as much as 23%. Making nightly lists of things one is grateful for improves the quality of sleep.

HEALTHY HEART

Recalling feelings of appreciation and listing things to be grateful for can protect the heart by decreasing blood pressure and lowering heart rate variability.

ACTION
Major STRONG

BREATHE EASIER

Grateful individuals avoid smoking, tobacco, thus avoiding a hard-to- kick habit that disturbs lung function and lowers life expectancy.

SLIMS DOWN

According to a study, grateful people exercise 36% more time per week and takes better care of their health overall.

32

THE GRATEFUL WORKPLACE

*With gratitude, work becomes an offering
of service, creating meaning and purpose.*

There were around a thousand employees in a previous organization that I worked at and the employee satisfaction ratio based on the ESAT score was 3.8. I decided to foster an attitude of gratitude at my workplace. I celebrated the gratitude week, during which, people wrote appreciation letters to each other and exchanged 'thank you' cards with everyone, including the support and security staff. We also had a Facebook page dedicated to further the culture of gratitude and create an atmosphere of goodwill, trust and mutual respect. After two months, the ESAT score went up to 4.2 and the company experienced a visible culture of gratitude. The productivity of a happy workplace propelled me to launch Seed of Gratitude, a venture that has transformed many corporate organizations into grateful workplaces.

A collectively grateful workplace can enhance employee engagement; build stronger work relationships, while fostering greater trust where people feel good about themselves and their work.

Research shows that organizations with high stress levels are low in gratitude and those low in gratitude have higher stress levels. The overall well-being and happiness of the workplace increases productivity. It is no secret that expressing gratitude to not only co-workers but outsiders - clients, vendors, and partners- helps to increase business.

Most employers are afraid to show gratitude to the employee for the fear of being asked for a higher salary. Most employees are afraid to show gratitude to their employer for the fear of being given more work or being taken for granted. Envy, jealousy and workplace politics generally discourage gratitude expression at the work place. Give employees more opportunities under employee engagement activities to express gratitude beyond the rewards and recognition programs. Monday blues can be cured if employee appreciation goes beyond the bell curve of salary appraisals.

A pay cheque is what motivates people at a very basic level. But we need to find meaning and purpose in our work, for which we are recognized and appreciated. Whether you are an employee, a leader, a trader or entrepreneur, see how you can build a grateful workplace. Even the smallest of gestures can make a big difference. Start small and build on your efforts. Bringing gratitude to work involves going beyond the hello curve, the typical rewards and recognition programs to incorporate gratitude as a value in the culture of the organization. Personalized gratitude letters, a gratitude zone with stickie notes, an appreciation box instead of a complaint box are practices you can bring to your workplace.

As companies focus on what is wrong and improvable to increase productivity and stakeholder value, it is important that they focus on what is right and appreciable to enhance employee satisfaction and create happier places for work.

A workplace that embraces gratitude as a value, appreciates

employees and their achievements. This is a factor that motivates employees to perform better. One of the biggest reasons for employee dissatisfaction is lack of recognition. Recognition and appreciation boosts self-esteem, in turn enhancing greater contribution at the workplace. Gratitude is also integral to the cultural quotient of an organization, especially in a global work environment to bring people and cultures closer.

Research suggests that 65 per cent employees quit their jobs because they feel unappreciated. Imagine the difference a simple 'thank you' can make even for the smallest of tasks.

Practice: Culture of Gratitude and Gratitude Week

Celebrate a 5-days gratitude week at the office

Day 1 - Start with gratitude letters that can be displayed on employee desks.

Day 2 - Sticky notes on a gratitude wall created at a common location where departments appreciate each other.

Day 3 - Pre-printed gratitude cards to give individually to every single employee in the office to extend the circle of gratitude.

Day 4 - Selfie zone and hash tag campaign to get people to take a selfie with their mentors, peers, colleagues and upload on social media to acknowledge them.

Day 5 - Keep the appreciation going with gratitude celebration and more letters, sticky notes, thank you cards for vendors, customers and stakeholders.

GRATITUDE
AT
WORK

**SEND THANK YOU NOTES
AND APPRECIATION NOTES**

Encourage your team to send thank-you
notes to others by equipping them with
sticky notes to share on a public board, or
engage in a we-basem that sends ecards.

MAKE A RECOGNITION BOARD

A large bulletin board in the breakroom
can be used for employees to post public
thank yous or other notes of appreciation
for all to see.

CELEBRATE TOGETHER

Whether it's for a birthday, national
holiday or a workplace milestine,
celebrations are a great way to show your
team gratitude.

SELFIE ZONE

Create a selfie zone where employees can take selfies with team
members and managers and
post them on intranet/internet.

GRATITUDE LETTERS

Encourage employees to
write letters of appreciation
for employee engagement
and team bonding.

DECORATIONS

Decorate the workspace with Thankfulness balloons, Gratitude as value posters,
danglers to provoke and encourage
employee gratefulness

**ENCOURAGE AND
REWARD INNOVATION**

By inviting your team to participate, ask
questions and make suggestions, you say,
"Thank you for being part of this team.
Your voice matters."

**OFFER WELLNESS
PROGRAM**

Wellness programs help your team feel
healthier and happier at work and when
they go home. You can offer rewards for
participating in wellness activities.

33

VITAMIN M FOR MONEY

Without contentment, the richest and the poorest
are in the same place of need and desire.

A few years ago, I spent a week in Auroville - a place near the south Indian city of Pondicherry - to learn permaculture, organic farming and vegan living. About 50,000 people from all over the world live here as an experiential community to realize human unity where interestingly, no money is circulated among people. Transactions take place through exchanging a task for a need and everyone supports the other for food and living, health and learning. I found that even with such a large group, gratitude can be an effective currency of sharing, loving and caring.

Most of us have a love/hate/guilt relationship with money. We love money, we hate not having enough of it, but we feel guilty when we receive more of it! If you have a grateful disposition, studies show that you are much more likely to learn from negative life events and translate that into a greater wealth.

I learnt a great deal in hindsight from my financial troubles in the past. What do you think will happen if you decide to enjoy your work in the midst of financial agony? You might sharpen your skills or get an inspiring idea, which can prompt you to work on something better than before. No one gets out of debt by thinking about debt. They get out of debt by being in a mind-frame to recognize opportunities for creating income.

While we think of money as a form of exchange, in reality we are exchanging energies and talents. Money happens to be a medium that facilitates this exchange. A lot of religions consider earning money on interest as a blasphemy for the reason money was meant to be a means of barter and exchange. But sometimes it becomes a medium of speculation, exploitation and greed. Like in the days of dotcom era and the current bitcoin rage, it is more about 'valuation' than about real value. We look at the idea of money as a symbol of true prosperity. Yet, what we essentially forget is that we have a limited time on earth and our true wealth is, in fact, a healthy good quality life.

The feeling of lack of something that we want is wired in our brains. We tend to view the world through the lens of this lack. However, the universe is the expression of abundance. By being in gratitude, we tend to be less materialistic, and probably spend less and save more. Grateful people are also generally more focused and productive - traits that certainly help with better careers and more money.

Do not let your situation become your identity. You may have lost money for decades, which may have led you to troubles, but is there something you can still be grateful for today? Start doing something different from today. It won't fix all your problems at once, but you'll start thinking differently and find newer solutions.

Often, we want things not because we love them but because we love the idea of owning them. Here we emphasize too much on the short-lived happiness of that feeling.

Instead of money, try using gratitude as a medium of exchange. In the words of cartographer and artist Fred De Witt Van Amburgh, "Gratitude is a currency that we can mint for ourselves, and spend without fear of bankruptcy." It is essentially the currency of joy that you pay to the universe.

As one of my teachers put it, empty what's filled with meditation, fill what's empty with intentions and scratch where it itches. Be grateful with all three.

Practice: Reverse Bucket List

Some people make a bucket list of things that they wish to accomplish before they die, places to travel, things to do, experiences etc. A reverse bucket list is the exact opposite - a list of things that you have already achieved.

Make a list of your achievements, however small or big. Don't belittle anything; everything is special even if it was done before. Instead of focusing on what you haven't achieved, acknowledge what we have already done.

Put this list together as a confidence booster when you are facing challenges at work or home or going through a bout of self-pity and or inadequacy.

Use the next page to make your quick reverse bucket list and expand on it, ever so often.

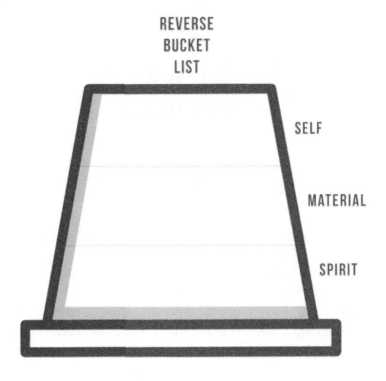

REVERSE
BUCKET
LIST

SELF

MATERIAL

SPIRIT

A bucket list is what you want to do before you die; a reverse bucket list is what you've already done and achieved. Celebrating your past is a quick and easy way to reconnect to how amazing you are already, regardless of what the future holds. Write a list of all the things you've accomplished that you are super proud of. Some big, others subtle. All which have played a part in crafting you into the super awesome person you already are.

Self : you, relationship, learnings, education
Material : work, money, achievements, possessions
Spirit : contribution, serving, experiences, fun

34

PAY IT FORWARD PARENTING

Children are our greatest teachers of gratitude.

When my daughter, Anamika, was growing up, I gained several valuable insights as a parent. It reminded me of how loving, kind and sacrificing my parents were. I truly understood and appreciated this when Anamika was a pre-adolescent and the choices I had to make for her best interests. In this balance of having a teenaged daughter and aging parents, I sensed what nurturing another life meant. We discover the meaning of life, when we love and give unconditionally, which is reciprocated without any expectations or obligations.

Teaching children the difference between wants and needs is important. Putting our needs ahead of our wants can put us on a path of gratitude. Children learn by absorbing and watching, so the best parenting lesson in gratitude is of complaining less and being more grateful.

I'm of the opinion that it is children who give us a chance to grow and evolve and also rediscover the love that our parents gave us. Parenting pushes the boundaries of patience and unconditional love. That is why parenting is a pay-it-forward initiative, paying to the next generation what we received in love and nurturing from our parents. In turn they will pay it forward to their children and so forth.

Children aren't an investment as is believed. Pay-it-forward parenting simply means that we nurture our children the way life has nurtured us. At a deeper level though, it is children who teach parents gratitude and not the other way around. If we raise our children with the attitude of gratitude, instead of entitlement, we can raise a happier and more optimistic society. Parenting is not just about our own children, it is also about the life we adopt to nurture, be it a student, a pet, or a garden.

One of the greatest gifts we can give as parents to our children is to hold back. In the process of trying to give everything, we tend to overindulge our children. As a result, children tend to become insensitive and less tolerant. I sent my daughter to a regular school instead of an international one with air-conditioned buses and class rooms. This was not because I couldn't afford it but because I believe that we must have more faith in them and let them be challenged. It's not easy to watch your kids struggle, but in the end, it does inculcate a sense of better appreciation for life in them.

Many parents would agree with me that it is not the easiest thing to raise a teenager. Hormones coupled with an environment of instant gratification can make being thankful rather difficult. As parents, this is the time to drive the values of grateful living and thankfulness by holding gratitude for the challenges these teenagers throw at us. It is an approach that can help us deal with these turbulent years for they are our biggest challenge and our greatest blessing.

Choosing to have a positive attitude in the house is an effective antidote to whining, jealousy, and complaining that is generated from within.

Give them experiential gifts, and not just toys or gadgets. You can present a membership to the children's museum, a library registration, or a camping trip. Experiential gifts build relationships, not materialism. Surprise them! Surprises help children see something as a gift, not an entitlement. Having too many choices breeds unhappiness- you are always wondering if you could have something better.

Ask your children, "What was the best part of your day that you are thankful for?" Older children can be initiated by parents to keep a gratitude journal.

Practice: Jar of Awesomeness and Gratitude Games

This practice is for individuals, families, groups, organizations and communities.

Decorate an old good jar and name it the Gratitude Jar. Whenever you see the jar, it opens the doors to your thinking about gratitude towards every relationship that you value. So, when you feel thankful, just put in some colorful gratitude notes in it. Read out all the notes aloud with your friends and family.

Dip into your childhood memories associated with play and joy.

Play gratitude games at home and work, which is an interesting way to encourage both adults and children to participate. A typical game can be Gratitude Pictionary where instead of drawing movie names, draw something that you are grateful to. Another popular game is "This Just In!" - Reporting your Blessings as a newscaster.

CONNECT
WITH
GRATITUDE

TIME
Grateful people on an average give 20% more time to their loved ones

COMMUNITY
Grateful people will have stronger relationships within local communities

FIGHTS *Grateful people get in to 30% fewer fights in their life*

EMOTIONS
Gratitude inculcates positive emotions that rejuvenate relationships for better

FRIENDS
Grateful people are more satisfied with others and are better liked

GRATEFUL
CONNECTIONS

Dysfunctional relationships are based on fear, guilt, shame and punishment. Gratitude brings us to connecting better from a place of love, kindness, compassion and unconditionality.

35

REDEFINING SUCCESS

Success is in the appreciation
of what we already have.

The dotcom bust had started at the end of 2000 that left my e-commerce company in doldrums. The stock market in the west crashed the following year with many investors committing suicide; a phase when I lost most of my personal wealth. Post 9/11, a downturn in our offshore supported business saw the last of my savings drain away. Over the next four years, I spiraled down rapidly and was also clinically depressed.

I eventually realized that Emotional Quotient (EQ) was more important than Intelligence Quotient (IQ). This opened me up to healing and self-help, redefining what success meant to me. But when I started seeing life more as an everyday improvement and appreciation of the journey, and of the people and circumstances in my path, I started improving my Gratitude Quotient (GQ). Beyond IQ and EQ, our GQ is something that we can measure and enhance by conscious practice and joyful effort.

Is money, status, fame, power equal to success? We know and understand that success means different things to different people. To some, success might be living a life of freedom or working to give back to the society or simply enjoying great health, although none of these might fit in exactly into the societal definition of success.

When you are grateful, success comes in many ways. You radiate positive energy and others like to be around you. Your appreciation includes and supports them. For instance, customers (and potential customers) love to feel that you are grateful for their business; it creates strong bonds of loyalty and mutual support. Employees are more committed and productive when they know that you are thankful to have them on your team.

Great resources and partners are attracted to you when they feel appreciated.

When you hold gratitude for what you have, you receive more and the more you receive, the more you open yourself to success. Here, we are not just talking about receiving in terms of money and materialism but also joy.

The Japanese concept of ikigai is defined as that which makes a person's life worthwhile, not just with money but anything that brings in satisfaction. It is believed that all beings have ikigai and with this, we know where our success lies in terms of important elements such as values, relationships, love and joy. My ikagi is in my entrepreneurship. I love the idea of business and the more I grow and learn, I am constantly amazed by the correlation between gratitude and success.

No matter where you are in your own life, you can enhance your circumstance significantly by simply focusing on being appreciative. Gratitude gives us the balance of saying I'm perfect and joyfully improving. Our most significant grateful growth comes from tapping into our support and facing new challenges.

Success in life is as important as success in work. A balanced view of success is composed of the eight essential elements of physical health, emotional well-being, relationships, materialistic wealth, spiritual growth, challenges, self-expression and our now ubiquitous relationship with technology. Success comes from consistently increasing the quality of our lives in each of these areas.

People who are grateful are aware of how wonderful life can indeed be because they appreciate and enjoy success, and when things don't go as planned, they put failure into perspective.

Practice: Success Visualization

Visualization is powerful tool that aids manifestation, stimulates our creativity and gives us a positive perspective to view life from. However, when it is difficult to visualize, try positive affirmations; these will programme the mind positively.

Involve all senses in your visualizations. Find a quiet corner for yourself and hold gratitude for your success, the way it comes most naturally to you. In vivid color, with stereo phonic sound, actually feel the thankfulness for the success; hear others appreciate it, and imagine the taste of it in your mouth. Visualize, add emotions and vocalize this experience.

Effective mental imagery should be very detailed. Soak in this experience with complete involvement and set the intention of the success and release it with a grateful breath.

GRATITUDE
FOR
FIVE SENSES

SIGHT

We have eyes because if we didn't, there would be no need for beauty, and no light, only darkness.

HEAR

Your ears are in charge of collecting sounds, processing them, and sending sound signals to your brain. And also help you keep your balance.

SMELL

The nose is the organ responsible for the sense of smell and also the maingate to the respiratory system.

TOUCH

We feel the cold, heat, contact, and pain. When someone touches us, "our brain can perceive it, appreciate it, and change it into a smile, a better mood, or some other friendly gesture.

TASTE

Taste buds are sensory organs that are found on your tongue and allow you to experience tastes that are sweet, salty, sour, and bitter.

In whatever capacity is our current perception through our senses, can we take a moment to be grateful for our senses with which we experience the world?

PART 6 : <u>**ⒶCTUALIZATION**</u>
BEING

Brother Monk

LIFE FULFILLMENT AS GRATEFUL BEING

Chapters

Needful Kindness

Full Mind or Mindful

The Smallest Prayer

Acceptance of Reality

Grateful Pause

Oneself to Oneness

Calm of Contentment

LIFE FULFILLMENT AS GRATEFUL BEING

Practices

Random acts of Kindness

Gratitude Meditation

Gratitude Prayers

Gratitude Walk

Stop, Look, Go Grateful (SLG)

Gratitude Connection

One Minute Gratefulness (OMG)

Brother Monk

36

NEEDFUL KINDNESS

Kindness, compassion and grace are the worldwide understood communication of gratitude.

I started on my project to create a gratitude kit that contains journals, list making notepads, gratitude letters, reminders, and keepsakes on living gratefully. I wanted the Dalai Lama to be the first one to receive it and give me his blessings for launching my MBT, Mission Billion Thanks, a mission that would ensure exchange of at least a billion thanks on this planet.

Meeting the Dalai Lama turned out to be a very emotional experience for me. He radiated immense compassion and peace. I felt blessed in his presence, handing over the first gratitude kit to him and seeking his blessings. On the day I met him, he spoke of kindness and it was a reiteration for me that everything we do can be done with kindness. It reminded me of the sign-off line in conventional letters that ended in "kindly do the needful". These words reflected hope and urge. This is also like a prayer.

Kindness to ourselves is something that we tend to forget when we put the needs of others ahead of our own. It is like the airline instruction asking passengers to put on their own masks before helping others. The first recipient of my kindness needs to be me. With compassion and kindness in our hearts, we can spread it outward at work and home. Being kind softens the heart and is the gateway to equanimity. This is a place from which we can serve others, doing what is appropriate and needful. The idea of seva in many Indian traditions is the concept of doing service for the sake of service without a reward, with an open heart.

Through acts of kindness and charity, we can restore the balance between what we receive and what we give away. This balance is what sustains humanity and its relationship with the world around. When we are thankful for what sustains us, we won't violate it. Generosity and random acts of kindness have helped me expand my circle of gratitude and are among the most beautiful practices you can take away from this book. Kindness towards the self and others through our words and deeds can raise our personal vibration, thereby enhancing the quality of our lives.

I have noticed that the ones in my circle that regularly practice random acts of kindness sometimes had a rather ambivalent relationship with their immediate families. It might be easy to be kind to strangers, but often requires courage to be kind to ourselves and our closest relationships. The idea is to appreciate these challenging relationships as well, and to draw strength from them as they hold up mirrors to our most intimate selves.

Practicing kindness makes us more positive and empathetic. Some might have regular charity rituals to make their life more meaningful, while others might be focused on earning good karma through kind acts. However, the karma may not flow back to you in the proportion and intensity with which you give something out. We can never really gauge the impact of our sharing. It isn't easy to tell which way the train went by looking at the tracks. Similarly, in the cycle of life and the nature of time, we can't always tell whether we're transacting forward or backward. Gratitude must be outside the idea of a transaction and without any expectations. Gratitude is a ripple and not a boomerang, in that sense.

One way in which you can meaningfully contribute to the world is by helping those around through random acts of kindness.

Practice: Random Acts of Kindness

Perform a random act of kindness for someone you know or for a stranger without expecting anything, such as buying a homeless person lunch.

The next time you order coffee, pay for the person behind you, or when you are at the drive through, pay an extra amount for the next person in line.

Donate your time at a food bank or animal shelter. Sharing your time with those in need can help put your own life in perspective.

Random acts of kindness, karma kitchens and paying it forward are all great exercises if done to truly extend the sphere of kindness to strangers and to people and circumstances that have no direct bearing on us.

RANDOM
ACTS OF
KINDNESS

An act of kindness is a spontaneous gesture of goodwill towards some-one or something - our fellow humans, the animal kingdom, and the kingdom of nature. Kind words and deeds come from a state of benevolence, generated by a core response deep within all of us.

173

37

FULL MIND OR MINDFUL

*Gratitude helps us focus on the
present moment and its beauty.*

Robert Emmons, one of the foremost scientists and researchers on gratitude and my all-time inspiration, recommends that focusing on individuals we are grateful for, as opposed to material things, will definitely get us in a better place. This ultimately creates wonderful forests of thankfulness.

My attempts at sharing my insights about gratitude were born out of the need to learn to be most grateful to lost relationships, to connections that faded away and to the newness of every moment. We generally teach what we must learn the most. My Mission Billion Thanks was inspired not because the planet needed to learn it but because I needed a 'goal Everest' kind of practice that would require a lifetime spent in grateful living.

Gratitude requires practice when it is easy and even more practice when it is difficult. The more we train ourselves to that end, the more we can fall back on it when it's most needed. This can be truly life-altering. Twenty one days of taking up any of these exercises and applying them to your life can certainly go a long way in upping your gratitude quotient. It will also help forge a deeper connection with life and enable you to view your story unfold in the larger context. It liberates you from the endless cycle of want and lack, opens your heart to kindness and forgiveness.

I would like to reiterate though, practicing gratitude is not being in denial of life's difficulties. Mindful gratitude alters your outlook to life by altering your perspectives to feel delight and wonderment at the things you already have. Once you are relaxed with where you are, it is far more harmonious to go where you want to.

Ask yourself what your 'gratitude ratio' is. Do you experience the pleasant things in your life in equal proportion to the not so pleasant ones? Do the bad things receive a disproportion-ate amount of your attention, such that you have a distorted sense of your life? When you look at how much you complain versus how thankful you are, you realize just how off the mark your emotional response is from the real situation.

As Zen master Suzuki Roshi says: To become mindful - which he also calls "beginner's mind" - is to see the world afresh without being lost in our reactions and judgments. In seeing it so, we begin to respond to the world than react to it.

Through the course of a day, there are several opportunities for us to live life in the best possible ways. The challenge is that we don't know how to do this. How can we remember to remember? Arrange to receive a gentle reminder several times throughout the day to pause, observe your thoughts, feelings and check if they are focused on gratitude or the lack of it? Use reminder prompts as discussed in the practices earlier.

Kindness to ourselves and pampering ourselves is something we forget in putting the needs of others ahead of our own like the airline warning about putting air masks on ourselves first before putting them on others in an emergency.

Being kind to softens our heart and is the gateway to equanimity. This is a place from which we can serve others doing what's appropriate and needful.

There are many examples we can see every day of selfless service without expectations if we open our heart. The idea of seva in many Indian traditions is the concept of doing service for the sake of service without a reward.

Practice: Gratitude Meditation

Gratitude meditation is an excellent way to start and keep up your practice of grateful living.

It is a form of meditation wherein we can focus on things that we are grateful for. In the beginning you can find a quiet corner to reflect and focus on all the people, things and situations that you are grateful for. Eventually you can extend this to include neutral and difficult people/situations.

A lot of videos on YouTube or Soundcloud are available for guided gratitude meditations and can be used initially to get you started.

Scientific research says that the benefits of consistent gratitude meditation are incredible to up our levels of joy and peace.

GRATITUDE
MINDFUL
REFLECTIONS

WHO AM I?

WHAT'S THE TRUE NATURE OF GRATITUDE?

Is gratitude a quality, a feeling, a mindset, an attitude?
Is it words of appreciation, language of thankfulness?
Is it a choice, positivity or spirituality?
What does 'being grateful' mean to you?

38

THE SMALLEST PRAYER

*The smallest and longest
prayer is thank you on a loop.*

Prayers have been a part of our rituals since our very existence. The ritual of prayers have included making sacrifices in the form of offering milk, wine, goats, coconuts, etc. Sacrifices are a way of giving back to the source from where we get them. The material possessions of these earthly beings aren't of great value to the idea of a benevolent god or the universe. They are only symbolic of sharing, an offering of thank you for what we get in abundance.

One of my closest friends is an atheist who believes that gratitude should be for people rather than for things and the creator. To him, the universe is a conglomeration of circumstances and coincidences without a purpose and no grand design or intelligence driving it. When I share with him how animals also show gratitude to each other, he admits that it is part of an evolutionary need to survive and procreate. But he can't fathom going beyond this idea. The only prayer he is willing to give is "thank you", and only for the immediate things that help and support him. I would say, even that can be the perfect starting point for one's gratitude journey.

He says, I am generally thankful for life. I recognize I am lucky and privileged in many ways. My appreciation is not directed towards a non-existent entity, but rather just to happenstance. I thank my mother for buying my first (second-hand) computer. My programming skills earned me money. I thank the many extremely talented people I worked with and studied under. I am thankful for my health. I had to undergo a surgery which went well because of the professionals in the hospital who were highly trained and well qualified. When I say that I am grateful for being alive, it's not for a god who created me, it's for the people in my life who helped me become the person I am today.

Richard Dawkins' book "The Selfish Gene" argues that all bio-logical and human behavior is in self-interest. French writer Francois de La Rochefoucauld says, "Gratitude in the generality of men is only a strong and secret desire of receiving greater favors." The German atheist Friedrich Nietzsche also mocked expressions of gratitude, saying they were disguises for seeking covert interests for gaining someone's loyalty. Hence, our expression of gratitude and prayers should be devoid of expectations and transactions and of altruistic nature.

To someone like me who does not have faith in a personal deity, but believes in a Grand Overall Design (GOD), a "thank you" is the smallest prayer I can give; most other prayers tend to be transaction of requests, demands and petitions for fulfilling desires. The yearning and our existential dilemma are something that drives us constantly. Some of us know, some doubt, some seek and some are plain disbelievers. No matter what's your inclination, gratitude is not dependent on any religious identity or belief.

Everyone is capable of a prayer called "thank you". As Eckhart

Tolle puts it - "if the only prayer you ever said is Thank you that will be enough".

One of my favorite spiritual poets, Rumi, says "you are not just the drop in the ocean, you are the mighty ocean in a drop", in tune with the 'Aham Brahmasmi' philosophy of Hinduism. Consciousness, pretending to play hide and seek with itself is a theme that many new age spiritual seekers talk of. Gratitude to self or the god within takes us on a path of recognizing the divinity of everything outside.

Practice: Gratitude Prayers

Incorporate thankfulness in prayers. Prayers need not depend on any religious beliefs or orientations.

Prayers are a form of saying thank you for everything. When you incorporate thankfulness in your prayers, it is natural to feel happier from within and more content with life.

While praying, it is helpful to light a lamp, a candle or any ritual that brings you peace. The flame of a candle or lamp symbolizes the journey from darkness to light and is a reminder of keeping the fire in us burning while recognizing the divinity in everyone and everything.

A lot of people practice ten thousand steps per day for physical well-being. Similarly, a practice of 100 Thank You prayers is a good idea for mental, emotional and spiritual well-being.

CO-CREATING
WITH
UNIVERSE

The concept of Amen, Inshallah, Thatatsu is that we can co-create along with the universe/god because we are given the choice of free will. Praying, asking and dreaming without joyful effort and practice are acts of laziness without true intention.

39

ACCEPTANCE OF REALITY

*Suffering is resisting reality; gratitude is
embracing it with deep acceptance.*

Suffering is very personal as it is based on our own view, our perspective of what is happening, and our own version of reality. During my days of depression and not much money, a negative mindset had set in. Life became a punishment with disinterest for most things and zero inclination to face reality. It was a vicious cycle that fed on itself. Medicines would give me short-lived relief, counseling did little to help. In deep exasperation and despair, I slashed my wrist and yet I survived, and how!

I transformed with the realization that external aids may inspire and motivate me, but the choice to change and count blessings beyond suffering comes only from within. One of my teachers introduced me to an idea that eventually turned into a life lesson for me. The definition of suffering is 'arguing with reality'. We suffer least when we accept rather than resist our present situation. Gratitude is the deep acceptance of reality.

You argue with reality each time you think that something shouldn't exist, when you are angry or upset about something that is happening to you, constantly thinking, "Why me?" This resistance is so chronic that some people truly do not know what it would be like to live without it.

We tend to live in so much denial of our here and now that we think, refusing to accept the truth will keep it from being true or that accepting means agreeing. Accepting doesn't mean agreeing. No one wants to live with pain, disappointment, sadness, or loss. However, you can stop suffering by practicing acceptance. Life is full of experiences that you enjoy and others that you dislike. But to accept it all as a part of life rather than want to choose only the good, leads to suffering. That is because you are resisting the present moment. Let an emotion come and go without holding on to it or resisting it. Avoiding emotions often leads to addictions, when you don't want to face up to your current reality.

We should do whatever is conceivable to make a situation better and at the same time approach it with as much acceptance and gratitude as possible. Start with what you can accept or feel grateful for in a situation - it gives the courage to accept and handle bigger challenges. The mind tends to see opposites as contradictory. "If I am truly accepting, then I can't fix the problem." However, if you delve a little deeper, you will discover the possibilities of accepting a problem and dealing with it positively. The effort you're putting in to overcome the problem is your learning. Be grateful to the problem for having taught you a new skill or discovering an inner strength.

Compassion for the self helps us avoid putting ourselves down, feeling worthless and self-doubt. Don't be okay with bad attitudes and behaviors, but accept that bad behaviors exist. We can choose to accept with compassion that negativity exists, leading to a feeling of gratitude. Even when it is impossible in a moment to accept or feel grateful, it is still possible to accept that you cannot accept. Start with what you can accept or feel grateful for in a situation - it gives energy to acceptance and eases the process of accepting the bigger situation.

The mind tends to see opposites as contradictory - "If I am truly accepting, then I can't fix the problem." However, if you delve a little deeper, you will discover possibilities of accepting a problem and dealing with it positively.

Practice: Gratitude Walk

Fundamentally Gratitude walk is a combination of two mood-busting and stress-busting life affirming tools being used together- walking and expressing gratitude simultaneously. Walk-preferably bare-foot - with a focus on things that you are grateful for and appreciate the things around you as you walk. Walking itself is a healthy exercise with numerous benefits and when coupled with a grateful state of mind, the impact can be miraculous for the body and the mind. This exercise can help you stay grounded and connect to reality as well as getting in tune with your creativity and intuition.

Take the practice beyond walking to repeating 'thank you' as a mantra in breathing exercises, counting crunches or sets in any other exercise.

INTEGRATION
OF
GRATITUDE

01

ATTENTION
The most precious gift we can give to anything.

AWARENESS
is what brings knowledge and true wisdom through the intellect.

02

03

ACTION
Doing the appropriate actions needed to get things done.

APPRECIATION
The verbal and written expression of our experiences.

04

05

ACCEPTANCE
The heartfelt emotion that sweetens our experiences.

ACTUALIZATION
The deep acceptance that syncronises all aspects of our existence.

06

Integrate Gratitude into your being by aligning your saying, thinking, knowing, feeling and doing

40

GRATEFUL PAUSE

*The pause of gratitude helps
us savor the essence of life.*

A company where I was heading the cloud computing technology division had started a new wing. This was the first time we were attempting to build a product, coming from a services background. Being a customer centric company, we had no background in running a product company driven by product features and release dates. The ultra-dynamic world of the apps ecosystem meant we were constantly strategizing and ideating over endless meetings, with hardly any sleep. It seemed like a task that would get us nowhere.

After months of frustration and disappointment, I took a break to attend Isha Yoga "Insight" - a spiritual and management retreat for CEOs of top companies in India. While in a conversation with the CEO of a large IT firm, I realized how difficult it was to transform from a services company to a product culture. This pause showed me how we were attempting to correct things without changing the basic nature of the company. After I went back, we compiled a list of things that we were grateful for. This was the first step. Eventually, we transformed the structure of our company and could make strides in developing a world class product. We move through life as though it is a theme park where we are on a day's vacation, trying to cram in maximum enjoyment, fleeting from experience to experience without a pause.

The pause allowed me to choose my responses to the stimuli in my life and make meaningful choices for critical decisions.

Many countries celebrate thanksgiving as a festival of gratitude for families to reunite. Most people use this time to reflect or give thanks. While such a celebration is an opportunity to rejoice, one should pause every so often even during the day and recognize at least one aspect of the day to be grateful for. Personally, I use my phone alarm to remind myself to take a break of what I call OMG - One Minute of Gratefulness. I sit for a minute in loving silence, sometimes with my eyes closed and give thanks to my tasks, to things around me, to my life and to my challenges as well. I also find myself getting more productive at work by doing so.

All of us wonder about what we must do to live a meaningful, fulfilling and balanced life. If our focus is on what we want, and what we have accumulated, we cannot find meaning and purpose. However, when we focus on being kind, compassionate and grateful, we find the best self-expression of our lives.

A few months ago, I did a Narmada parikrama program, which involved walking for eight days, a distance of about 150 km - sometimes bare foot - carrying a 10 kg rucksack along the banks of the river Narmada in Gujarat on rough terrain, without a phone or money, depending on the seva and food offered by people on the way, mostly not venturing into civilization. This exercise of deprivation and pushing my physical, emotional and mental limits, combined with daily meditation and reflection had a profound impact of resetting my expectations from life to zero. We ate food offered to us on the path by the generosity of strangers; we were led and shown the path through wilderness, jungles and farms when lost late at night.

Back to civilization after this pause of an ascetic experience, small pleasures, mercies of good food, clothes, the warmth of friendship, making love, technology; I look at all of these as the blessings that they truly are.

Practice: Stop, Look, Go Gratitude (SLG)

From Brother David Steindl-Rast, the Benedictine monk.

Stop: Be quiet. In that calm, take in every moment or situation as a gift to be grateful for. Can we take a moment and be still? What benefits might we experience if we do?

Look: Be curious about your own experience in this moment. What do you see? Hear? Feel? For what can you experience a sense of gratitude? Perhaps you just remember that you are alive. That there is no moment exactly like this moment.

Go: Living is an art that you create as you go. What seed for action is this moment offering you? How can you make it beautiful for yourself? For others? Ask yourself these questions and wait patiently for an answer. When you get one, do it, act on the insight that comes.

CIRCLE
OF
LIFE

ONENESS

HARMONY

COMPASSION

BALANCE

CONNECTION

JOY

POSITIVITY

∞ ACTUALIZATION
Monk. GRATITUDE

Gratitude is finding the balance with bias towards positivity in things. Joy is in being grateful, happiness beyond a reason or season. Gratitude shifts us towards the oneness of all things and includes them in our world. Gratitude connects us to the circle of life. It gives us the harmony required for peaceful coexistence.

41

ONESELF TO ONENESS

Gratitude shifts us from one-self to one-ness.

For someone who always found meditation a struggle, I confused belonging and bonding to the idea of oneness. A bout of antibiotics and considerable damage to my digestive tract actually woke me up to how wonderful an ecosystem the human body is and how interconnected our entire world is. When I was in the hospital for a few days, I realized how dependent I was on others for everything. As I started being grateful to my family who would sleep in the hospital room, my friends who kept me company during the day and the nurses who cared for me far beyond their duty, I got a glimpse into how connected we are to our atmosphere, to the bacteria that live within us and the web of human connections.

In my meetings and interactions, I found people who would be introduced to me as self- made. When talking about their journey, they would acknowledge the amazing set of circumstances, technologies, people and choices that helped them succeed, leading me to understand that self-made was just a myth and we are too amazingly supported by the universe.

When we become more aware of the realities beyond ourselves, we get rid of illusions of being self-made. After all, we co-create our circumstances with others and the universe. The more grateful we are, the more the universe helps us co-create.

From plants and animals to the air that we breathe, there are things that we are completely dependent upon for our survival and propagation. Gratitude gets us to acknowledge, accept and appreciate this interdependence and moves us from the idea of oneself to oneness.

As a seeker too, I found gratitude to be the most meaningful practice of my life. I saw many of my friends living gratefully. Their passion and connectedness to their art and self-expression or to the people around them was indeed inspiring. I realized that their gratitude to life might not be a prayer or thanking ritual. But their self-expression through whatever gift they are blessed with is their way of serving the world and everything around them.

Gratitude took me away from being self-centered and egoistic, to knowing how I was connected to everything. The kernel of gratitude is in all of us since each of us experiences life as an individual. The practice of gratitude doesn't take away self-centrality. Instead, it can take you away from an ego-focused attitude to include everyone and everything that has contributed to making you who you are.

To me, this interconnectedness is oneness. Sometimes a glorious sunset or a sky full of stars, spectacles that took my breath away and when time seemed to stop, making me feel one with everything. We have felt it sometime or the other; however it is so fleeting that many fail to catch it and many find it difficult to sustain it. This is similar to my experience of being timeless and formless that I experience in the gap between my thoughts during meditation. To quote Russell Brand: "It's difficult to believe in yourself because the idea of self is an artificial construction. You are, in fact, part of the glorious oneness of the universe.

Everything beautiful in the world is within you".

Gratitude and humility help us look at life beyond ourselves. Our awareness of our limitations and the sense of human co-dependence become keener and not confined to the limited ideas of the self. As I move ahead on this journey of finding true oneness, I know the path to it is through gratitude.

Practice: Gratitude Connection

Acknowledging and appreciating grateful connections will keep your relations strong. Think of any person or thing you would like to establish a connection with. Feel one with it by mentally connecting to it.

Now affirm these words, "I feel you", "I see you", "I love you", "I'm one with you". This mindful reflection will help us move from a state of "Oneself" to "Oneness".

This practice can be tried particularly with objects or people you might dislike or have difficulty dealing with. I have used this exercise with my daughter who was afraid of dogs. Today, she feels far less agitated with a dog around and is at least able to approach one with a bit more confidence.

ONESELF
TO
ONENESS

I see you
I hear you
I feel you
I know you
I connect to you
I love you
I'm one with you

We can mindfully connect to something by giving it all our senses, emotions and connecting to it fully whether it is an object, person, circumstances or relationship. When we move beyond the self made and me, myself attitude to giving credit to people, circumstances and the world around us, we move to seeing the truth of interconnectedness and to the idea of oneness. Gratitude shifts us from oneself to oneness.

42

CALM OF CONTENTMENT

Contentment is acknowledging abundance
of the universe and what we have.

In my quest for self-discovery, I realized that our worth should be based on the belief that what we are and what we have is enough. This gratefulness can lead to a state of joy, a better quality of life, and peace. Life's satisfaction comes from living a grateful life.

The materialistic world bombards messages about acquisitions in life - riches, gadgets, luxury etc. These often lead to feelings of unhappiness, anxiety, lack and a false sense of entitlement. It deprives our mind of the deep stillness which the soul yearns.

This sheer need for survival is also the reason for our mindless accumulation of things to protect us from lack and scarcity. Since lack and scarcity are so ingrained in our being over millions of years of evolution, our natural instinct is to look at what we do not have and want a future where we will not need anything. To go against this programming and look at what's right, what we can be content with and to reign in our desires is a skill that will come through consistent gratitude practice.

The challenge is to decide how much is enough to live a life of contentment. Everyone is unique in the way they undertake the journey towards fulfillment. If there is one thing that makes an enriching companion, it is gratitude. To be truly content in everyday life, it is necessary to balance needs, hopes and desires with blessings that you already have received, much beyond your expectations and imagination. The art of gratitude teaches you how to be appreciative and content with blessings - those you yearn for and those you haven't even considered.

I'm a goal-oriented person, from something as small as finishing a task on time in a day to running multiple companies. And once I've achieved a goal, I begin looking for another.

Does this say that I'm not content with my life? Not at all. On the contrary, I'm extremely content with my life and all that I've got. I have accepted that I am someone who will always strive to reach a goal, enjoys a new challenge. But what matters most to me is the journey that gets me to the goal. And I'm content with being that type of a person.

Contentment isn't a matter of being complacent with your situation and never trying to improve it. It's a matter of being content with what you have right now and building on what there is rather than complaining about what isn't. While being discontent is the cause of several unhealthy habits, contentment is the cure and gratitude is the pathway to it.

As a technology entrepreneur, I am used to the idea of planned obsolescence. If you've been at the receiving end of this with the latest launch of your favorite phone every quarter, don't be surprised! Exploiting the natural propensity of the brain for newer and better experiences, marketers use this phenomenon to ensure that we are always looking for more.

Buddhist and Jain monks usually carry a bowl big enough for just a meal; there is nothing to hoard or save for a rainy day. The bowl represents the limit of what they can have, and what the bowl can contain. They don't expect, ask, or seek more. As there is no expectation, there is no complaining and desire for more. They are content with what they have.

Gratitude is a measure of our perspective on the things we already have. Contentment is a measure of our perspective on things we don't have.

Practice: One Minute Gratefulness (OMG)

Choose any practice of pausing and reflecting and do it for one minute at the desk, in the car, at the dining table or at home. Use a timer app for gratitude breaks to steer your mind back to an attitude of gratitude.

Get up from your chair and find someone to smile at. Just pause, close your eyes and before going into a meeting, consider the best possible out-come and be grateful for it. This will help you ensure the success of whatever you are going to face next.

Make a mental list for one minute to be grateful to, e.g. pick an alphabet, and decide a place, people, circumstances, events, places, things.

ONE MINUTE
OF
GRATEFULNESS

One Minute of Gratefulness can be practiced anytime, anywhere; in the middle of a workday while sitting in your chair, in your bed, at your favourite space – just pause whatever you are doing, take a one minute break. Refresh yourself with gratitude. Just breathe in, hold it and slowly release it, rhythmic consistent full breaths concentrating on all things that you are grateful for.

ENTREPRENEUR

SPEAKER, AUTHOR

GRATITUDE COACH

Prashant went from being Bankrupt, Depressed and Suicidal to living a Magical life of Fulfilment through the power of Gratitude. The book, Vitamin G: Gratitude juxtaposes his intensely personal journey how he lost and found myself with 42 Gratitude practices and how you can apply it to yours for Joy, Abundance and Life Fulfilment.

A DAGSI Scholar from Wright State University, USA with a Masters in Computer Science, Prashant went from selling his company for a million USD to Softbank and JP Morgan at age 24, to witnessing the tumble of the stock market crash, the dotcom bust and the 9/11 aftermath besides being diagnosed as clinically depressed.

From attempting suicide twice facing adversity and challenges in health, relationships and finances, he is back to living a fulfilled magical life with joy and abundance, successfully running multiple businesses in e-commerce and cloud computing, to gifting solutions and Wellness.

He attributes this transformation to gratitude and Grateful Living. He has made his life purpose to magnify joy through raising gratitude consciousness across the world.

✻ *Gratitude Life Coaching*   *Speaking Engagements* ✻
✻ *Grateful Shift Training*   *Workshops* ✻
✻ *Invidual One To One Sessions*   *Retreats* ✻

Gratitude Week
Culture of Gratitude Business Transformation
Grateful Cities

All proceeds from these engagements go to
the Seed of Gratitude Foundation for charity.

www.prashantjain.in
Email : contact@prashantjain.in
www.linkedin.com/in/prashantindiadomain
www.facebook.com/smilepj

BIBLIOGRAPHY

I have quoted many authors and their books in this book, their practices and methods are copyrighted by them and are quoted in the book with attribution to them.

A lot of the scientific research is from Greater Good Science Center at University of California Berkeley that has contributed immensely to the study of gratitude and many others like them.

The quotes by many authors, philosophers, thinkers are attributed and I would suggest further reading of the original sources as below:

ArrienAngeles: Living in Gratitude

Dr. BJ Fogg: Tiny Habits method

Douglas Adams: The Hitchhikers Guide to the Galaxy

Eckhart Tolle: The Power of Now and A New Earth:

Awakening to your Life's Purpose

Elisabeth Kubler-Ross: On Death and Dying Gary Chapman: The Five Love Languages series Marcus Aurelius: The Meditations Marsha Richins and Scott Dawson: Measuring Material Values:

A Preliminary Report of Scale Development Nick Vujicic:

Life without Limits: Inspiration for a Ridiculously Good

Nithya Shanti: The Joyshop Workbook

Pastor Will Bowen: A Complaint Free World

Richard Dawkins: The Selfish Gene Rhonda Byrne: The Secret

Robert Emmons Ph.D : Gratitude Works,

Thanks! How the New Science of Gratitude Can Make You Happier,

The Little Book of Gratitude

Simon Sinek: Start With Why: How Great Leaders Inspire Everyone to Take Action

Sujith Ravindran: 7 spiritual laws of abundance

Anthony Robbins, David Steindl-Rast, Fred De Witt Van Amburgh, Francois de La Rochefoucauld, Friedrich Nietzsche, Maya Angelou, Oprah Winfrey, Russell Brand, William Arthur, Voltaire, Zen master Suzuki Roshi

Journal of Personality and Social Psychology

Readers are requested to kindly bring to our notice any resources or discrepancies in quoted source material

http://www.prashantjain.in
contact@prashantjain.in
http://www.facebook.com/groups/circleofgratitude

Made in the USA
Coppell, TX
19 January 2025

44616948R00121